Crackle Glass

in color
Depression to '70s

With Price Guide

Leslie Piña

Photography by Leslie & Ramón Piña

Schiffer Publishing Ltd

4880 Lower Valley Road, Atglen, PA 19310 USA

Designed by Leslie Piña
Photography by Leslie and Ramón Piña
Layout by Bonnie M. Henlsey
Type set in Swis721 BT

ISBN: 0-7643-1136-0
Printed in China
1 2 3 4

Published by Schiffer Publishing Ltd.
4880 Lower Valley Road
Atglen, PA 19310
Phone: (610) 593-1777; Fax: (610) 593-2002
E-mail: Schifferbk@aol.com
Please visit our web site catalog at **www.schifferbooks.com**

In Europe, Schiffer books are distributed by Bushwood Books
6 Marksbury Avenue Kew Gardens
Surrey TW9 4JF England
Phone: 44 (0)208-392-8585; Fax: 44 (0)208-392-9876
E-mail: Bushwd@aol.com
Free postage in the UK., Europe; air mail at cost.

This book may be purchased from the publisher.
Include $3.95 for shipping. Please try your bookstore first.
We are always looking for people to write books on new and related subjects.
If you have an idea for a book please contact us at the above address.
You may write for a free catalog.

Dedication

for the West Virginian glass workers

Acknowledgments

As always, many kind and generous people contributed to this project: Lee Allen of Antiques Downtown, Washington, Pennsylvania; Mitchell Attenson of Attenson Antiques, Cleveland Heights, Ohio; Richard Blenko of Blenko Glass Co.; Aimee Bolt (cracklegirl), Richard and Virginia Distel, Myra Fortlage, Ed Goshe, Chris Hatten; Huntington Museum of Art, Huntington, West Virginia; Hansel Jividen, Robert McKeand; Seneca County Museum, Tiffin, Ohio; and Sheila Randel.

Libraries that were especially helpful include the Rakow library of the Corning Museum of Glass, the Huntington Museum of Art Library, Cleveland Public Library, and the Ursuline College Library. Thanks again to Peter and Nancy Schiffer, Douglas Congdon-Martin, and the Schiffer gang.

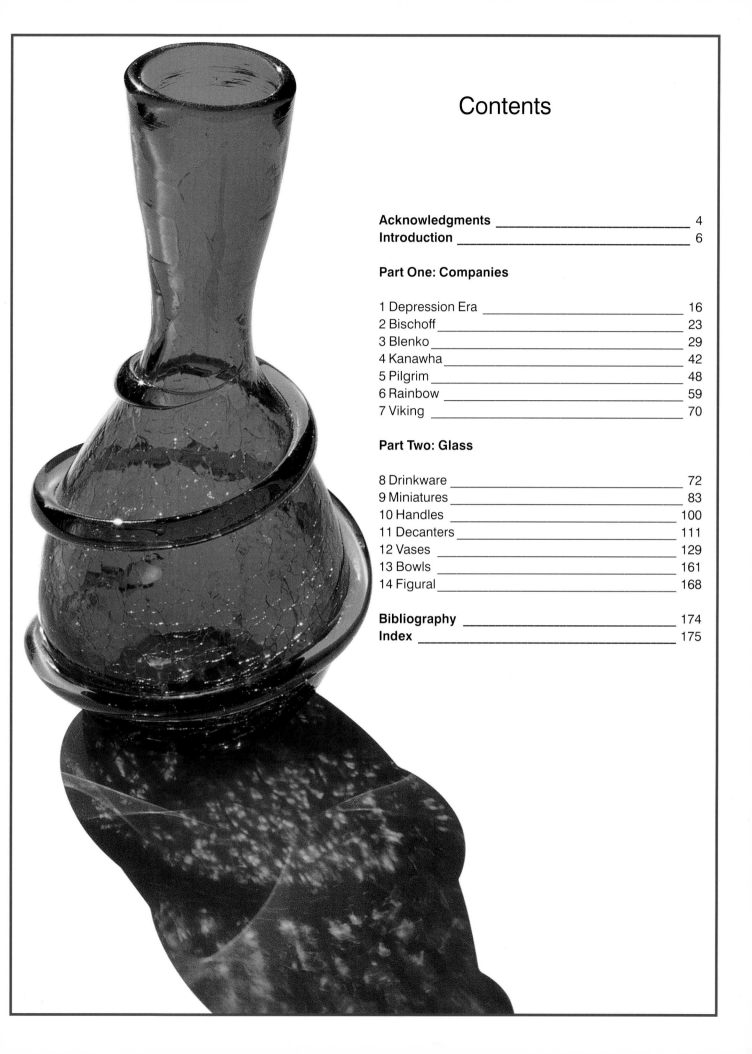

Contents

Introduction

Crackle glass is not a style; it is not by any particular designer or company; it is not from any one period of time. Crackle is a finish added to the glass to give it a cracked or crackled overall texture. This finish affects neither the color nor the form of the piece. In fact, many designs, such as by Blenko, could be ordered in either plain or crackle finish. The latter is added while the piece is hot, by immersing it in cold water. Sudden and extreme change in temperature shocks the glass and causes it to crack. It is then reheated to smooth and strengthen it, leaving irregular lines of crackling.

Because collectors of crackle glass focus on this special finish, collections are widely varied — from miniatures or "window" pieces in traditional forms, to big modern designer pieces. Generally, the small common examples command very reasonable prices, even though they are usually mouth-blown and hand-made. On the high end of the range are the Blenko pieces from the '50s and '60s sought after by other collectors. Mid-century modern enthusiasts often accessorize with these large brilliantly colored pieces. And as might be expected, many of these designer pieces were copied (both carefully and badly) by several of the contemporary glass factories. It is this category of direct copies and close imitations that can be challenging. Attribution can be almost impossible if the copy is good, but there is usually some qualitative difference in addition to overall appearance. By comparison, the original design will usually stand apart.

Dozens of companies made crackle glass at one time or another, but during the years from about the late 1930s to the 1970s, five West Virginia companies produced the majority of all crackle glass on the market today. Blenko, Pilgrim, Rainbow, Bischoff, and Kanawha (and to a lesser extent, Viking) were responsible for most of the colorful crackle glass seen at flea markets, shows, shops, malls, and on the internet. Other companies, like Hamon, Empire, Heritage, and Bonita, made crackle glass, but without labels or published catalogs, these can be difficult to identify.

In addition to these factories, some of the large so-called Depression era companies made a limited amount of crackle glass. Fry made some very early items; Tiffin made some unusual two-color items; Duncan made some crackle for Raymor around 1950; and even Imperial made some crackle tumblers. These Ohio and Pennsylvania companies only made crackle as a novelty or an extension of their regular lines of hand-made but not mouth-blown Depression era glass. The state known for off-hand (mouth-blown) glass, including crackle, is definitely West Virginia.

Generally, the majority of the miniature vases, pitchers, and jugs were made by Pilgrim and Rainbow. Blenko made very few lines of miniatures, and these were usually little versions of regular-sized items in the line. These modern shapes are among the easiest to identify of all the miniatures. Others, such as those by Rainbow, Pilgrim, or Kanawha can be confused with each other. Bischoff copies muddy the water further.

Most extremely large stoppered bottles, pitchers, and unique designs were designed by Wayne Husted from 1952 to 1962. Distinguishable from both Blenko's early tableware designs and the modern forms introduced by their first in-house designer, Winslow Anderson (designed 1947 to 1952 and less known for crackle), these Husted pieces have given Blenko its reputation as the leading producer of big colorful fifties glass. He was succeeded in 1963 by Joel Myers, who followed Husted's lead plus introduced other memorable modern designs. Few of these outstanding designs were attempted by other companies, with the exception of Pilgrim designs by the Moretti brothers, Alessandro and Roberto. But Moretti designs introduced Murano style to Pilgrim rather than items suitable for crackle.

Blenko models that were widely copied include the pinched ivy vases, a variety of pitchers, early stoppered bottles, and Anderson's bent-neck decanter. The other companies also introduced lines made to compete with, rather than copy, Blenko. Pilgrim had lines with satin finish, peachblow coloration, speckles, Murano-styled animal figurines, and heavy cased pieces. Kanawha, usually distinguishable by its traditional forms and a molded foot rather than a pontil mark, also made cased items with white interiors and bright exteriors. Besides their blatant knock-offs, Bischoff produced some of the most bizarre forms of all. But all of these West Virginia companies were responsible for the crackle glass made during the mid-century decades that fascinates collectors. Those still in business, notably Blenko and Pilgrim, still produce crackle glass. It can be easily distinguished from other new crackle glass — from the cheap molded items made in China and other countries, to one-of-a-kind studio pieces.

With increased interest in vintage crackle, prices have risen, sometimes dramatically. Rather than rely on prices

Catalog page showing Swedish crackle. Although crackle glass is usually thought of as a West Virginian product, it was also made elsewhere. *Courtesy of the Huntington Museum of Art.*

Crackle is a decorative effect used on ceramics as well, as seen on this Zsolnay vase from Hungary with heavy textural crackle.

Kanawha and Pilgrim, two West Virginian companies known for their crackle miniatures, also made other products. These Kanawha cased and Pilgrim satin glass pitchers were very popular items.

from various publications or asking prices from sales sources, I have focused more on actual selling prices in compiling the value guide. For example, although miniatures have been valued much higher by some, they normally sell in a modest range. Size is very important — the bigger the better, according to most collectors. Generic pieces with no particular designer or even company attribution also command lower prices than comparable items that can be identified. Labels are desirable, but they should not be relied upon too heavily; paper labels are very easy to transfer. Relative rarity will affect price, perhaps more than other criteria. Some of Husted's designs for Blenko, for example, were produced for a very short time. Conversely, some early (1930s or 1940s) Blenko designs remained in the line for decades and are common today. A common piece, even of quality design and craftsmanship, will be less valuable than a rare item. Some of the least common de-

signs were unusual forms that were more costly to produce. These also happen to be among the most collectible, because of both rarity and fascination with the unusual.

Since prices for crackle glass vary so widely and change so quickly, this guide will probably be outdated by the time the book goes to press. But as a guide, its purpose is simply to help distinguish between the desirable and the less desirable pieces. *Neither the author nor the publisher can be responsible for any outcomes from consulting this guide.* Both, however, wish you luck in the chase and enjoyment with the find.

Most of the crackle glass shown in the following pages was made by the off-hand method. In 1976, as part of the Bicentennial celebration, the Huntington Museum of Art produced a series of booklets called *New American Glass: Focus West Virginia.* The following is reprinted with minor modifications *courtesy of the Huntington Museum of Art.*

Blenko made many of their designs with either a plain or a crackle finish, but decanter stoppers were generally plain, as shown in this group.

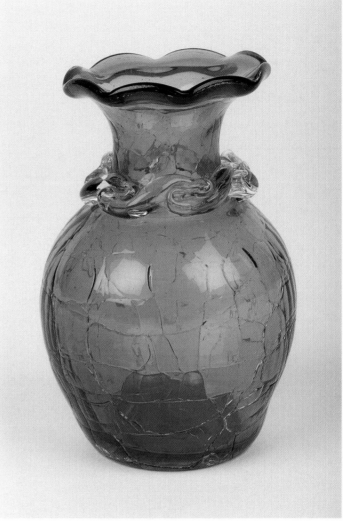

Top left: Blenko stopper with crackle finish.

Left: Cheap molded reproductions with cut rims, made in China.

Top right: Cranberry is a popular Pilgrim color today. This new miniature vase can be dated by this color.

Above & opposite page
Crackle is also used on some late Blenko designs, as seen in these examples by
Blenko designer Matt Carter in 1997. *Photos courtesy of Matt Carter.*

The Glassblowing Process

Glass is formed in nature by volcanic fusion of sand, or silica. Man-made glass, fused through heat, has been in use for over 4000 years. Egypt, Mesopotamia, Syria, Persia, France, Italy, Germany, England, and America all have long traditions in producing glass for utility and ornament. Throughout its history, the way in which glass is blown has changed very little.

The initial step in glassblowing is the melting of the ingredients in a clay pot placed in a furnace. A recipe of sand and other chemicals, called a *batch,* may be mixed with broken fragments known as *cullet* and heated to a temperature in excess of 2500 degrees Fahrenheit. It can be worked and blown at a lower temperature, but in its working state, the glass resembles thick honey, and it will still be too hot to be touched with the hands.

Glass is not naturally colored, so metallic oxides must be added as the glass is melted. For example, copper oxide makes either a red or an aqua glass color, cobalt a blue, manganese a purple, and cadmium sulfide a yellow glass. Each of these compounds must be added to molten glass in a separate furnace to prevent colors from running together.

Since the glassblower can never touch the glass, his tools serve as fingers and hands to shape and pull the hot ball of glass. The blowpipe is his main tool. This is a hollow steel rod about 54 inches long with a blowing end and a flared end for gathering the glass from the furnace. The flared end is placed into the mouth of the furnace and heated until it glows faintly. This is necessary, because molten glass, or *metal,* will not stick to the end of a cold pipe. After the pipe is hot, the glassblower lays the end on top of the hot molten glass in the furnace. The pipe is rotated carefully, *gathering* a gob of glass — an action that is difficult to master, because just the right amount of glass must be gathered on the pipe.

Gathering. *Photo courtesy of Blenko.*

The pipe must be continually rotated to prevent the newly gathered glass from running off the blowpipe.

As the glassblower leaves the furnace with the hot gather of glass on the pipe, he must keep the pipe turning while he walks to his work area. Learning to balance the blowpipe and keep the glass in motion is tricky. Any jerky or awkward movement may break the momentum and shift the gather from the center of the pipe — making it more difficult to blow.

Back at his work area, the glassblower decides whether to *block* or *marver* the glass. Blocking is done at the bench using a fruitwood block into which has been carved a hollowed circle or oval. The blocks are kept in water while not in use to keep them from cracking. To block the glass, the blower rests the blowpipe on the elongated arms of his bench, pulls one of the blocks from a bucket of water, and places the hot glass gently on the block. Rolling the pipe back and forth, the glass is rotated inside the block. This procedure assures that the gather is evenly centered on the pipe.

After blocking or marvering, the first bubble is formed by blowing air into the end of the blowpipe. Only a small puff is necessary, because too much will blow the bubble walls too thin. The glassblower may rest the pipe on the end of the bench arm while he blows, or he may blow it in the air. The way in which the pipe is held is unimportant, as long as the blower can watch the bubble as it begins to swell out. Again, the glassblower must be sure to keep the pipe turning or the bubble may blow unevenly. He must also see that the glass is not getting too cool. Although it may not be glowing as red as originally gathered, the glass must be kept at a hot working temperature, or it could crack and fall of the pipe before the piece is finished.

To reheat the glass, the blower places it into the *glory hole,* an aperture in a furnace and dips the pipe back into the glass furnace for a second gather. This is accomplished by rolling the pipe with hot glass from the first gather, around and around in the molten glass in the furnace. The larger ball must also be marvered or blocked to center it on the pipe. This process may be repeated until the desired amount of glass is accumulated.

Now that the ball or *parison* is larger, the glassblower may make decorative additions to it by gathering a bit of colored glass from a different furnace onto a second pipe, laying it on the piece and snipping it off with shears which will cut right through the hot flowing glass. The glassblower may also take hot glass threads and wind them around the parison. A tool resembling an ice pick can be used to pull the threads in several directions, providing a surface decoration similar to that seen in many Tiffany-style pieces. Decoration can also be added by rolling the piece across a layer of slender glass rods placed on the marvering table, which then fuse to the piece. These decorative elements are then melted onto the main surface by placing the piece back into the glory hole. As it reheats, the new colors and elements form a smooth surface with the original parison.

Before the glass is blown out too thin, the glassblower must be sure to *jack* the piece. Back at the bench, he takes a tool called *jacks* and gently squeezes near the end or neck. As the piece is rolled up and down the arms of the bench, the gentle pressure on the hot glass will leave a slightly indented ring. Later, this ring will be important in cracking the piece off the blowpipe.

The glassblower has now made several gathers, marvered and/or blocked the

Making adjustments. *Photo courtesy of Blenko.*

piece, and perhaps added designs and/or color. Now the blower can shape the piece by reheating it, holding it straight down towards the floor, and swinging it out or around his head or gently swaying it from side to side. These movements will pull the piece out into a longer or flatter shape.

At this point the vessel is a closed shape, because the neck is still attached to the blowpipe. To obtain its final form, the glassblower must transfer the piece to another pipe

called a *punty* or *pontil rod*. This is a metal rod about five feet long and solid, since no more blowing will occur after the transfer. To transfer the piece to the punty, the glassblower reheats it, returns to the bench, takes a wooden paddle or *battledore,* and rotates the end of the piece against the paddle. This action flattens the end slightly, forming the bottom of the piece and providing a smooth surface for attaching the punty. Meanwhile, an assistant heats the punty in the furnace and gathers a small gob of glass onto the end. This gather is removed from the furnace, taken to the marvering plate, and flattened to form a blunt end.

The flat bit of glass on the punty is stuck onto the smooth bottom of the piece. This is a critical step, since too much pressure could force the bit through the bottom, and too little pressure could result in failure to bond the glass. When the two pieces are secure, the glassblower takes a wet file and scores the piece with a sawing motion around the indentation made by the jacks. The blowpipe is then separated from the piece by tapping it near the head, leaving the piece attached only to the punty.

Still secured to the punty, the glassblower returns to the furnace for reheating before working the end that was broken off from the blowpipe. Still fairly thick and rough in appearance, the reheated end can be smoothed and reworked back at the bench. The glassblower may expand the opening with jacks, cut it off with shears, or lay a wrap of hot glass around it to make a lip, depending on the desired design. Handles may be added by taking a small gather or *bit* of glass on another pipe, laying the bit on the piece, cutting it, pulling it out, and pressing it back onto the surface. Handles are added late in the process, because too much reheating would soften them too much or cause them to collapse.

All of the finishing touches are completed as the glassblower gets ready to crack the piece off the punty and place it in an annealing oven. The *crack off* is done with a tool, usually at the end of a file, and the piece is eased onto a table covered with two or three inches of a soft non-flammable material, such as vermiculite. The piece is picked up with a fireproof glove and placed into a warmed oven for annealing. This is a process that reduces the temperature of the glass gradually, keeping the exterior and interior temperature of the piece equal. This slow, even cooling to room temperature is critical, because any sudden change in temperature will cause the glass to crack. The final annealing process may take several hours or longer, depending on the thickness of the piece.

The preceding describes only *off-hand* techniques. Another commonly used method is mold blowing, in which the molten glass ball is blown into a wooden or metal mold. As air is blown through the blowpipe, the glass is forced into the shape of the mold. When it is lifted out, or the mold removed from around the glass, the piece bears the shape and any surface decoration from the mold. Since molds are intended to be reused, they are ideal for creating exact copies or series. Whether made off-hand or mold blown, glass is always a blend of the designer's creativity and the craftsman's technical virtuosity.

Glossary

Batch. Mixture of raw materials to be melted into glass; also known as *mix.*

Blocking. Shaping a gather of glass in a hollowed block to give it a symmetrical form.

Blowpipe. Hollow iron tube two to six feet long, used to gather and blow glass.

Crackle. Finishing technique of submersing hot glass into cold water to create an overall surface of fine cracks.

Cullet. Glass fragments that are cleaned and added to the batch.

Gaffer. Master glassblower.

Gatherer. Person who gathers molten glass from the furnace.

Gathering. Removing glass from the furnace on a pipe or punty.

Glass. An organic substance formed from a mixture of compounds that fuse into a mass that cools into a rigid condition without crystallization.

Glory hole. Opening in the furnace, or separate furnace, used for reheating glass to make it workable.

Jacks. Tool used to form glass, made of spring steel, usually with two metal blades connected to the top.

Lehr. Annealing oven where the temperature of finished glass is reduced gradually.

Marvering. Rolling a gather of glass on a flat surface (formerly of marble) to give it a symmetrical form.

Melt. Molten glass in the furnace.

Metal. Molten glass.

Mix. Batch.

Mold blown. Formation of glass object by blowing it into a mold.

Off-hand, free blown. Formation of glass object by blowing and manipulating tools, without the use of molds.

Pot. Crucible, usually of clay, in which glass is melted in the furnace.

Pressed. Molded glass that is pressed into a mold by mechanical means.

Punty, pontil rod. Solid iron rod used to gather glass and to hold a vessel during finishing stages.

Servitor. First assistant to the gaffer.

Shop. Unit of three to five workers in a factory.

Taker-in. Person who takes finished glass to the annealing oven or lehr.

Tooling. Shaping, marking, or decorating soft glass with the use of hand tools.

Hot ball of glass. *Photo courtesy of Blenko.*

Shearing. *Photo courtesy of Blenko.*

Part I: Companies

Chapter 1
Depression Era

The tri-state area of Ohio, (western) Pennsylvania, and West Virginia is known for having produced most of what is commonly called Depression Era glass. Unlike inexpensive pressed and unpolished "Depression glass" (the similarity of these terms can be confusing), Depression *Era* glass is relatively costly, made by hand, and polished. Both types were made during the Depression of the 1930s, plus about a decade before and after that period.

Crackle finish was not ordinarily used for Depression Era glass. Instead, companies like Fostoria, Duncan, Morgantown, and Tiffin, decorated by methods such as etching, cutting, staining, enameling, gilding, and applying contrasting colors of glass. Some of these companies, however, also produced a limited amount of crackle glass, and they often advertised in trade journals like *China, Glass, and Lamps.* Weatherman's book on Depression Era glass includes several of these and other advertisements from the 1920s that provide information on this crackle output: Westmoreland advertised what they called "Scramble" beverage sets in 1924; Macbeth-Evans patented a jug in 1927 and used crackle on some other items; in 1928 Federal showed different "Jack Frost" crackled beverage sets for iced tea, water, and lemonade; McKee featured crackled beverage sets, console sets, and cheese & cracker sets in 1929; L.E. Smith called theirs "By Cracky"; Fry made several crackle items before closing in 1933; Morgantown made some footed wines and similar items; Duncan made their Raymor Connoisseur crackle about 1950; and Tiffin made several crackled beverage items in the 1920s and Guild Gossamer crackle in 1938.

There were also examples of crackle glass made by other companies during the period loosely called the Depression Era. Blenko, which is one of the major producers of mid-century crackle glass, began to introduce it in the 1940s, still considered part of the Depression Era as the term is used by glass collectors. Though by no means a Depression Era company, Blenko is included in this chapter as an example of overlapping styles of glass during same period, but by very different kinds of companies.

Catalog page from Huntington Tumbler Company showing crackle glass. *Courtesy of the Huntington Museum of Art.*

Left: Left, unidentified stem with crystal crackle bowl and green foot; right, Morgantown wine glasses, also with green foot. 3-1/2" h.

Right: "Faux crackle" made by L.E. Smith Glass Company in the late 1920s. *Courtesy of Mitchell Attenson.*

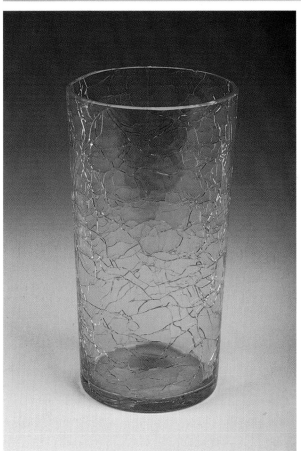

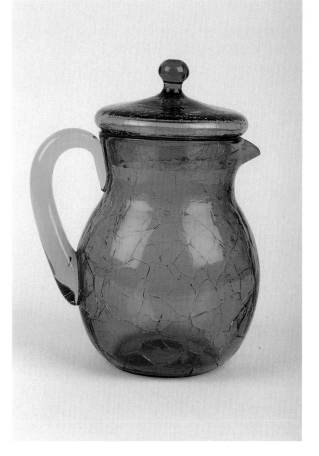

Top: Tiffin #517, 12-oz. Tumbler in Canary; with #117, 64-oz. Covered Jug in Canary with Blue trim. *Courtesy of Ed Goshe.* $25-35; $300-350
Bottom left: Detail of Tumbler.
Bottom right: Tiffin #117, 64-oz. Covered Jug in Blue with Canary Trim, one of the items featured in *China, Glass, and Lamps* in 1924. *Courtesy of Ed Goshe.* $300-350

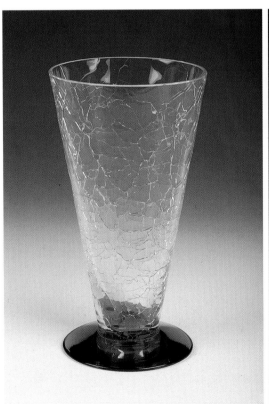

Top: Tiffin #14194, 2-qt. Jug with cover in Crystal with Green trim; #14185, Ice Tea in Crystal with Amber trim; and #14194, 2-qt. Jug with cover in Crystal with Amber trim. *Courtesy of Ed Goshe.* $225-275 each jug; $20-30
Bottom left: Detail of #14185 Ice Tea.
Bottom right: Right, #117, 64-oz. Covered Jug in Crystal with Green trim, with cased glass finial (shown with #14194 Jug). *Courtesy of Ed Goshe.* $200-250

Tiffin Guild Gossamer Tumbler in Crystal. *Courtesy of Seneca County Museum. $45-65*

Tiffin also made limited crackle (called craquel or cracquelled) in their modern designs of the 1940s and 1950s. This Crystal Sweet Pea Vase is from the #17430 line produced c. 1945-1970. 6" h. *Courtesy of Ed Goshe. $150-175*

Tiffin Guild Gossamer Handled Jug in Crystal, designed by R.R. Kostellow and patented in 1938, signed Victor Hendryx (worked at Factory R 1909-1938). 12-3/4" h. *Courtesy of Richard and Virginia Distel. $500-600*

Green Imperial crackle tumbler
with twisted sides. $10-20

Avocado Imperial crackle tumblers,
shown with brighter green. $10-20 each

Blenko was one of the major companies to make crackle glass from the 1950s-1970s, but they began making it by the 1940s. Some of the designs were from the "Depression Era" of the 1930s, like this #39 ivy vase, shown in typical Blenko vivid colors. $20-30 each

Top: Blenko #390 vase with flared fluted top, in Amethyst. $50-60

Bottom: Blenko #366 vases shown in 10-inch Turquoise (Blenko Blue) and 7-inch blue with applied leaves. $40-50; $50-60

Detail.

Duncan crackle glass is very unusual, as seen in this Raymor Connoisseur line
designed by Ben Seibel and distributed by Richards and Morgenthau (Raymor)
in New York. Shown are Avacado 3-part relish dish and 14-1/2 in. serving dish.
$50-60 each

Raymor Connoisseur tumbler and 6-1/2 in.
mayonnaise/dressing with ladle, also in Avacado.
$15-20; $40-50

Chapter 2

Bischoff

A.F. Bischoff Glass Co. in Culloden (began 1922) made items very similar to those of other West Virginian companies. In addition to using some unusual, even bizarre, original shapes, Bischoff copied designs from leaders like Blenko. Copying, an undeniably common practice, has been responsible for a great deal of confusion in identifying and dating both crackle and plain blown glass of this period. Although each company had distinctive items (Blenko certainly contributed the greatest number of original designs), many shapes were imitations of what was seen elsewhere. Some of these copies were executed well and looked very good — perhaps just as good or even better than the originals. Since a considerable amount of skill and effort is involved in executing both a knock-off and an original design, it is curious that more originals were not made. For example, a version of the pinched #39 ivy vase introduced in 1939 by Blenko, was also produced by several other companies. The shape is a simple one and could easily have been modified by its imitators. Yet in most cases, they chose to make the same shape. And where Blenko may not have copied neighboring companies, there is an unmistakable similarity between many of their designs and those made in Murano, Italy at the same time. However, the influence could have flowed in more than one direction.

Lancaster Colony, of Columbus, Ohio, purchased Bischoff in 1963, keeping the Bischoff name and molds.

(Blenko's fifties glass designer, Wayne Husted, joined Lancaster in that year to head its design and production department.) The following year, 1964, Sloan Glass bought Bischoff, and Sloan closed in 1996.

Many of the Bischoff items on the following catalog pages bear a striking resemblance to Blenko designs. In some cases they are modified enough to prevent confusion. Bischoff's #720 bamboo-like shape was undoubtedly inspired by Husted's design from the 1950s; but it is quite different. Similarly, neither Bischoff's #906 gurgle bottle nor #591 bent-neck model would be confused with Blenko designs — Husted's gurgle decanter or Anderson's famous bent-neck decanter (both of which were also copied by Pilgrim). The punch set, another Blenko copy, differs enough in color and form to identify it as Bischoff. But other items are more direct copies: the #328 small jug, #900 large jug, and #411 dented vase would be more difficult to attribute without a label.

Of course not all Bischoff designs are unoriginal. In fact, many can be recognized by a distinct style that these designs seem to share. Exaggerated forms, complicated ruffles, bumps, and baubles, crystal stoppers and handles, and generally heavier look seem to characterize the company's product. Novelty rather than modern design seems to have been the focus.

Bischoff labels.

Bischoff catalog pages. Bischoff made plain clear, opaque cased, and crackle finish glass. Shapes were often copies or interpretations of designs by Blenko and other companies. *Courtesy of the Huntington Museum of Art*

excitingly inspired...   *delightfully different...*

delicately designed...

traditionally true...

Bischoff!

519-6" 519-5" 519L 519M 519S

241S 401

128 241M 241L

30S 33S 32S 31S 31M

GLASS MARBLES GLASS CHIPS 290 294

440

407

430 PAPPAS BROTHERS 380 PUNCH SET 127

126 108L 108M 108S 948

910 297 720 221 467 719

969 729 478 973

101 287 920 943

8P 471 240L 34½ 115

240M 240S 229

922 800 330 452 822

282 281 1185 118M 118L

103 A-13 100 124

841 820

245 324 961 107 967 974

819 510½

957 109 510 708 832 937

724   972   975   117   945   120

556   811   959

255   971   986   962   914

949   825   453   416   906

987   213   990

431   122   821   942   152   214

992   237   730   905   831   912

900   215   944   375   104   970

Chapter 3

Blenko

Blenko Glass Co., along the Mud River running through Milton, West Virginia, began by making stained glass for windows. Although today it is better known for colorful oversized bottles and an assortment of decorative items, Blenko still rolls out flat glass from large cylinders and remains the major American producer of "antique" stained glass for architectural installations.

When William John Blenko (1855-1933) left London in 1893, his goal was to make and market handmade stained glass in the United States. At that time only machine-made "cathedral" glass was being made in the United States, while handmade glass was imported from Europe. Blenko believed that he could place quality over quantity and make a niche for himself by offering antique stained glass in the United States at competitive prices.

After several failures, and at age sixty-seven, a weary Blenko made a final try at Milton, West Virginia, calling his modest plant Eureka Glass Company. Blenko tried to persuade his younger son William H. to join him, but aside from financial help from William and his brother Walter, the elder Blenko was in it alone. The next year however, in 1923, William H. (Bill) joined his father in Milton. As if Blenko hadn't had enough trouble, the Crash of 1929 had a profound effect on stained glass usage. Bill's idea to expand into decorative wares — vases, bottles, and the like — proved to be both a quick fix and the first step toward later success. Blenko's considerable knowledge of chemistry and experience with formulating colors could be applied to the new line of decorative wares.

Two Swedish-American glassworkers from the Huntington Tumbler Co., Louis and Axel Muller, agreed to work at Blenko part-time in the evenings. Their skills at glassmaking and at teaching local workers proved invaluable. Now that Blenko had the idea, the facilities, and the skills in place, he needed a mechanism for marketing. A German immigrant by the name of Eddie Rubel had a talent for sales and a New York-based company called Rubel and Fenton. Rubel was the perfect choice for an agent, especially since New York was the critical location for distribution, but Blenko had other representatives such as Robert Pierce in Chicago, Reginald Markham in Texas and California, and Dillon-Wells.

Unlike the original stained glass, the decorative wares attracted consumers, and major department and specialty stores featured them. Crackle finish was an option on some of these popular Blenko designs — designated by the letter "C" in the model number. Both large and small crackle

was used, so Blenko crackle items are identified in the same way as plain Blenko — by form and by color. Although crackle glass doesn't appear in the catalog until 1946, it was probably made a little earlier, especially on their popular lines with applied leaves or rosettes.

The only Blenko pieces that might be difficult to identify are closely copied designs, such as Anderson's bent-neck decanter. Most Blenko crackle is easy to identify, especially if it appears in catalogs. A number of these catalogs are readily available, because they have been reprinted. Miniatures, generally the most troublesome crackle items to identify, are easy to attribute to Blenko. The company produced very few miniatures, and those were in modern shapes mimicking their full-sized counterparts. But the most impressive and collectible crackle pieces are the larger vases, pitchers, and decanters — the designer pieces by the fifties and sixties trio: Winslow Anderson, Wayne Husted, and Joel Myers.

Winslow Anderson

In 1946 Winslow Anderson became Blenko's first full-time designer. He was born in Plymouth, Massachusetts in

Early silver foil hand label used on Blenko pieces through the 1970s.

1917, where he remained through high school graduation. Anderson graduated from the New York State College of Ceramics at Alfred University with a B.F.A. in ceramic design in 1946 (his studies were interrupted by a four-year stint in the Army during World War II).

Although he considered himself to be a craft potter, Anderson joined Blenko in 1947 and introduced many wonderful modern designs, some of which won national awards. In 1952 Anderson left Blenko for the Lenox China Company in Trenton, New Jersey. Lenox had offered him the position on four occasions, and Anderson refused each time. "Finally," he said, "they made an offer you'd have to be a bloody moron to turn down." Since Lenox purchased the Brice Glassware Company in Mt. Pleasant, Pennsylvania, Anderson was able to continue working with glass in addition to designing china. Since retiring in 1979 he has been dividing his time between his sailboat off Long Island, traveling, or at his house in Milton, West Virginia. In 1999 the Huntington Museum of Art, in Huntington, West Virginia, held a retrospective exhibit of Anderson's Blenko. A half-century after their creation, these modern shapes and colors are as refreshing as if they had been introduced today.

Wayne Husted

Born in 1927 in Hudson, New York, Husted graduated from Hudson high school in 1945 at the end of World War II. He studied at Alfred University from 1947 to 1952 and graduated with B.A. in English and both a B.F.A. and an M.F.A. in Industrial Ceramic Design. Husted joined Blenko on April Fools Day of 1952 and stayed as Design Director until January, 1963, after designing the 1963 line. In addition to the hundreds of new designs Husted introduced during those years, he was responsible for the photography and design of the Blenko catalogs. One of his designs won an award in the Corning Museum of Glass competition and was featured in the now-classic catalog *Glass 1959.*

After leaving Blenko, Husted was Director of Design and Product Development for Lancaster Colony and for the next ten years designed products in every material from glass to plastics, from rubber to metal. He also designed for Viking Glass and Anchor Hocking. He continues to design internationally and resides in California. But among Blenko collectors, Husted is most admired for introducing the colorful oversized bottles and decanters that have made such a statement for both Blenko and American fifties glass.

Joel Philip Myers

Myers was born in Peterson, New Jersey, in 1934. After studying advertising design at the Parsons School of Design from 1951 to 1954, he graduated with honors. He then studied ceramic design in Denmark 1957-58, and he earned a B.F.A. and M.F.A. from the New York State College of Ceramics at Alfred University in 1963.

Like Anderson and Husted before him, Myers came from Alfred without training in glass and took his first job at Blenko.

But unlike his predecessors, Myers also learned how to blow glass during his tenure as Blenko's design director from 1963 to 1970. Heavy airtwist stoppers, elongated forms, two-color designs with applied spirals, and textured surfaces are some of Myer's contributions.

In addition to his being one of the pioneers of the American studio glass movement, in 1970 Myers began teaching art, glass, and ceramics at Illinois State University, where he founded the Glass Department. By the time he retired from his position as Professor Emeritus in 1997, Myers had won numerous awards, seen his work included in museums throughout the world, and had left a legacy as an important twentieth-century glass artist. He continues to work in his home studio in Pennsylvania.

John Nickerson

Nickerson, born in 1939, was Blenko's forth design director and second studio glass artist. After earning a B.S. degree from Montana State University, he went on to get an M.F.A. from Alfred University in 1969. He then served as Blenko's design director from 1970 to 1974. Since Blenko produced most of its crackle in the 1950s and 1960s, Nickerson was not known for many crackle items. Among his most admired designs was the 1972 Charisma line of crystal vases, bowls, and decanters internally decorated with random red swirls.

After the mid-century era, Blenko continued to produce off-hand glass under the direction of Don Shepherd (1974-88), Hank Adams (1988-94), Chris Gibbons (1994-1995), and Matt Carter (1995 to present). Crackle glass is still being made in both crystal with applied decoration and colors.

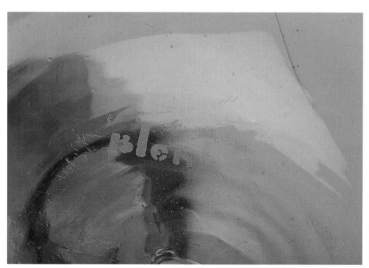

Sandblasted (not acid-etched) signature, designed by Wayne Husted, and used on his and some earlier designs produced only in 1959 and 1960. This signature was used to distinguish Blenko from the many copies being made. It was soon discontinued, because it proved to be uneconomical

Late Blenko cellophane label.

Small crackle on Blenko (Pilgrim is known for using small crackle).

Large crackle on Blenko.

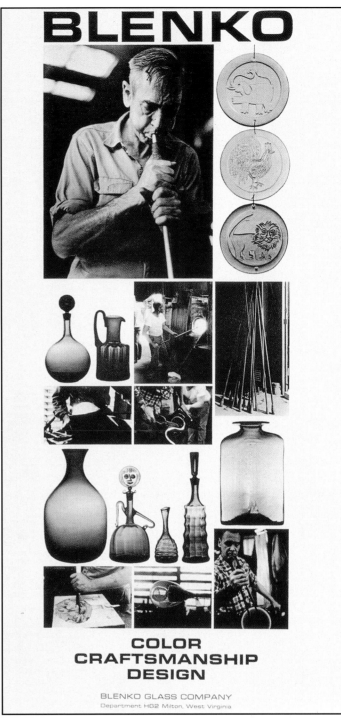

Advertisement for Blenko glass showing glass workers and 1960's designs. *Photo courtesy of Blenko.*

Brochure with exterior and interior view of Blenko factory.

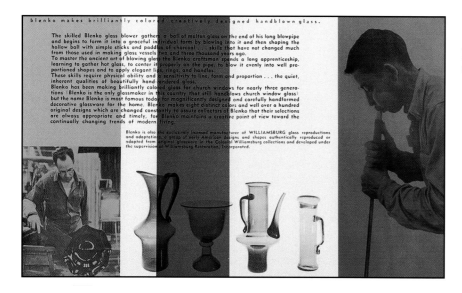

Brochure showing glass blower and examples of Blenko glass.

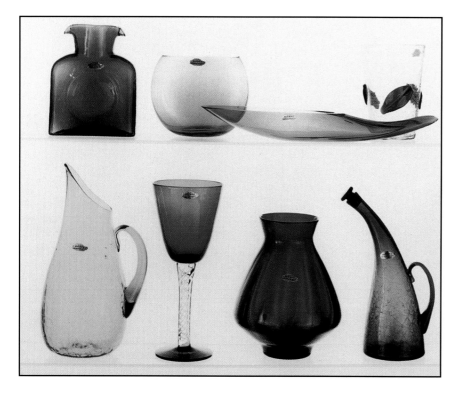

Photo for Blenko advertisement with designs by Winslow Anderson c. 1950. *Courtesy of Blenko.*

Blenko showroom, 1950s.
Photo courtesy of Blenko.

Blenko factory, 1950s. *Photo courtesy of Blenko.*

Blenko Visitor Center.

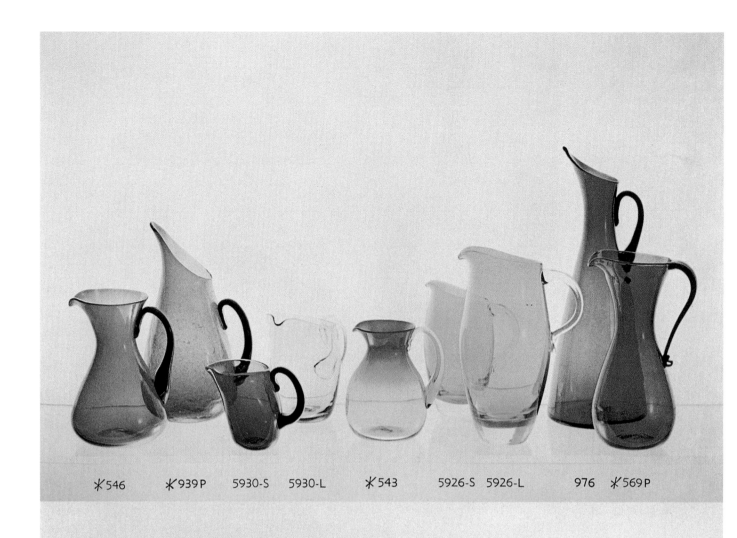

✳546   ✳939P   5930-S   5930-L   ✳543   5926-S   5926-L   976   ✳569P

598-L   598-M   598-S   991   579   ✳361-P   ✳3750-L   571-0   586

Blenko catalog pages. The first two digits of the item number indicate the year of the design; the following digit(s) indicate the design number. An asterisk by a number means that the design was also available in crackle.

11

6

51L Bubbles (Only)
6" dia.
$24.00 doz.

*626L
22" high
$12.00

*626M
16¾" high
$7.50

*3744X
7" dia.
$3.50

6224L
10½" high
$7.00

6224S
7½" high
$5.00

5433
10" high
$12.00

639
14" high
$7.00

6520
18" high
$9.00

*6515
13½" high
$6.50

*388
7½" high
$6.00

955L
17½" long
$7.50

*366M
9½" high
$5.50

*366L
12" high
$7.00

*6323L
12½" high
$6.00

*6323M
9" high
$5.00

*6323S
6" high
$4.00

971M
16" long
$15.00

971L
25" long
$30.00

971S
12½" long
$8.00

6217
21½" high
$7.50

6529
20" high
$11.00

6521
14" high
$9.00

*636S
8" high
$5.00

*636L
11" high
$7.00

*6143S
5½" dia.
$1.20 ea.

16143L
10½" dia.
$4.50

*6311L
21¾" high
$9.00

*656L
14" high
$8.00

*656M
10½" high
$6.00

*656S
8½" high
$5.00

*6517
10" high
$6.00

*418S
4½" high
$2.00 ea.

*418L
6" high
$2.00 ea.

*6526
15¾" high
$9.00

*627L
18" high
$7.00

*627S
12" high
$5.00

3434
5½" high
$6.00 pr.

647
17" high
$10.00

648
19" high
$11.00

*6211
15¼" high
$10.00

*3744X
7" dia.
$3.50

*657S
12" high
$5.50

*657M
14" high
$7.50

*657L
18½" high
$9.00

657LL
22¾" high
$11.50

6519
16½" high
$14.00

6522
6½" high
$4.00

6523
10¼" high
$5.00

*6533
17¼" high
$9.00

*654
11½" high
$6.00

†643
8" dia.
$4.00

*6027
17" high
$10.00

6224S
7½" high
$5.00

6224L
10⅜" high
$7.00

*6514
14¼" high
$7.50

991
13½" high
$7.50

6532
14½" high
$10.00

*629
8½" high
$8.00

*629S
6" high
$6.50

*366L
12" high
$7.00

*366M
9½" high
$6.00

6710B
9½" high
turquoise/olive only
$9.00

6710A
9½" high
tangerine/honey only
$9.00

6027
17" high
$10.00

5815M
23½" high
$12.00

6416
14¼" high
$7.50

644
11" high
$5.00 plus F.E.T.

*6524L
17" high
$9.00

*6524S
13" high
$7.00

*6528S
24" high
$8.00

*6528L
31" high
$10.00

6741
crystal stoppers only
with Lemon or
Tangerine Bottles
23¼" high
$13.50

6742
11¾" high
$8.00

6740
15½" high
$9.00

6320
3¾" dia.
$5.50

6321
4¼" dia.
$4.50

*666A
5½" dia.
$1.50

666B
4½" high
$4.00

644
11" high
$6.00

38

12

6513
6" dia.
$7.50

B508
6½" dia.
$6.00

6716
14¼" high
$12.00
Crystal Stopper with
Lemon or Tangerine
Bottle

*6424
5" high
$3.00

*6726
9½" high
$8.00

*6721S
12¾" high
$8.00

6722
14" high
$7.00

6415
12½" high
$7.50

*6427
24" high
$7.50

6115L
14½" high
$7.50

*990
12" high
$7.00

*990A
3⅛" dia.
$1.00 ea.

*6734
16½" high
$7.50

*6685
6½" high
$5.50

*6512
6" high
$6.00

*6726
9½" high
$9.00

*3750L
5½" high
$5.50

6511
9½" high
$6.00

*6714
5¾" high
$8.00

*418S
4½" high
$2.00

*418L
6" high
$2.00

6911
7½" high
$3.00

*6365
8" high
$6.00

6912
10" high
$6.00

*6944
9½" high
$8.00

*64B
13" high
$3.00

6945
6½" high
$3.00

64D
11" high
$3.00

*6630S
8½" high
$6.50

6913
Approx.
11½" high
$3.00

*6424
5" high
$3.00

660
8½" high
$6.50

384
7½" high
$3.00

6926
Approx.
7" high
$16.00 pr.

*699A
6½" high
$6.50 pr.

*6813
7" high
$6.50 pr.

*6725
3½" high
3½" wide
$6.50 pr.

*699B
6½" high
$6.50 pr.

*434
5½" high
$6.50 pr.

6511
9½" high
$6.00

7013
5½" high
$6.00

*3750L
5½" high
$5.50

6910
6¼" high
$5.50

7014
6¾" high
$6.50

*6714
9¼" high
$8.00

*418S
4½" high
$2.00

*418L
6" high
$2.00

*6516
14½" high
$8.50

*636S
8" high
$6.00

669
8½" high
$6.50

7019
11¾" high
$7.50

7018
13¾" high
$6.50

6912
10" high
$6.00

708
7⅝" high
$4.00

*6630S
8⅝" high
$6.50

*6944
9½" high
$6.00

6913
approx.
11½" high
$3.00

64D
11" high
$3.00

*64B
13" high
$3.00

705
6½" high
$3.00

*6424
5" high
$3.00

6911
7½" high
$3.00

704
6" high
$3.00

6945
6¾" high
$3.00

707
6½" high
$4.00

*976
19½" high
$10.00

991
13½" high
$7.50

*37
13" high
$6.50

6214
11" high
$6.00

6214
11" high
$6.00

*628S
24⅝" high
$9.00

*49
10½" high
$6.50

*627S
12" high
$4.50

627L
18" high
$7.00

629L
10½" high
$11.00

629
8⅛" high
$7.00

*629S
6" high
$5.00

*6122M
21½" high
$8.50

*6122S
16½" high
$7.00

*6122L
26¾" high
$12.50

5925

＊5519-L ＊5519-M

＊366-SL ＊366-ML ＊366-LL

"818L
9¼" high
½ gal.
approx.

"818S
6½" high
1 qt.
approx.

"418L
6" high

7911L
10" high
crystal
&
wheat only
½ gal. approx.

7911S
6" high
crystal &
wheat only
1 qt. approx.

"745
6" high

"7818
6¼" high

"7315
10" high

"418S
4½" high

"7116
6½" high

"3750L
5½" high

＊404-M ＊404-S ＊404-L ＊366-S ＊366-M ＊366-L

8

7727S
15" high

789S
12¾" high

8138
14" high

7738
16" high
crystal wheat & ant. grn.

41

Kanawha

When Dunbar Glass Co. in Dunbar, West Virginia closed in 1953, the production head, D.P. Merritt, and others joined to form the Kanawha Glass Specialties Co. Named after a nearby river, the Kanawha, the company opened in 1955 and made blown crystal in addition to cutting and decorating purchased glass. In 1957 they changed the name to Kanawha Glass Company. By 1960 they began production of the colorful decorative wares that have become so familiar, especially crackle glass. Soon Kanawha was making 350 production items in seven colors.

In 1969 Kanawha purchased Hamon Handcrafted Glass in Scott Depot, West Virginia. Hamon had begun in 1932, and their crackle glass production during the 1950s and 1960s coincided with that of other companies. The Hamon crackle glass that was added to the Kanawha line retained its identity, which explains why Kanawha catalogs often show two different types of glass — molded and hand blown.

In the early 1970s, cased milk glass was introduced, in which the outer (or sometimes inner) layer was made in bright solid colors. "Peachblow," with gradations resembling the nineteenth-century art glass by that name, was

one of the most popular of these cased lines. Production continued until 1987, when Kanawha was sold to Raymond Dereume Glass Inc., in Punxsutawney, Pennsylvania. This lasted for only two years, closing in 1989.

Of Kanawha's crackle glass production, it is the #85 amberina pitcher with the stretched spout that most people are familiar with. It is also one of, if not the only, modern design. The many Kanawha miniatures, with ruffled rims or applied squiggles look like the countless traditional designs by any one of the companies making crackle miniatures. Larger Kanawha items also copy or interpret designs by other companies: the tall stretched bud vases resemble some Viking or Fenton items: the #148 double-spout water bottle is the Blenko design with a molded motif; #1163 and #1166 ruffled bowls, and # 1168 crimped bowl are also Blenko knock-offs; the #1165 swan bowl is taken from Duncan. Whether borrowing from history or from contemporary factories, Kanawha designs can often be identified by the molded foot and visible seams. Their Hamon production is more challenging, since these hand blown pieces can be mistaken for the work of other companies as well.

Kanawha label.

Detail of typical Kanawha bottom, with molded foot and no pontil mark.

Kanawha catalog pages with emphasis on their crackle items.

Ruby #1

1126 1128 1123 1121 1125 1122 1127 1124

Ruby #2
1131 1129 1130

Ruby #5
1140 1142 1141 1143 1145 1144

Ruby #3
1133 1132 1134

Ruby #4
1138 1137 1139

291 148 21

290 885 22

44 31

43 830

1091

710

715

85

719

367

6-8H

205

888

1087

6-8

42

880

86

402

842

809

393

390

45

Pitcher #1

Pitcher #2

Vase #1

888

42

809

1087

393

86

6-8

880

402

842

390

291

148

21

290

885

22

44

31

43

830

Chapter 5

Pilgrim

One of the few remaining factories responsible for crackle and other hand-made glass, the Pilgrim Glass Corporation of Ceredo, West Virginia is headed today by the man who founded it in 1949. Alfred E. Knobler was trained as a ceramic engineer and entered the glass business via pottery sales in the 1930s. During World War II he worked for the War Department as an engineer, but soon returned to pottery and glass sales.

Tri-State Glass of Huntington, West Virginia was headed by Walter Bailey, who at that time was going through a difficult time. Knobler believed that he could turn around the failing company, so in 1949 he purchased it from Bailey. After the addition of a new gas line into the company, Knobler's belief turned into a reality, and success prompted him to expand. After purchasing land in Ceredo (near Huntington) he built the present Pilgrim facility and opened it in 1956. Shortly after, the Corning Museum of Glass featured one of Knobler's designs in its *Glass 1959*.

From the beginning they specialized in free blown crackle glass in vivid colors. Colors listed in the 1951 catalog were Amber, Blue, Chartreuse, Crystal, and Emerald Green. The fine "onion" crackle that Pilgrim is known for, is made in the same way as other larger crackle — by dipping the hot glass object in cold water, which causes it to crack in random patterns over the entire surface. The piece is then reheated to smooth the surface, but the fine crackle lines remain as part of the design. Like other producers of crackle glass, Pilgrim made large quantities of it in the 1950s and 1960s. Generally, they used colored handles in the 1950s and crystal handles in the 1960s. Some items can be identified as Pilgrim by a mark impressed in the center of the base — either a group of little dots or a group of parallel wavy lines.

Like other companies in the area, Pilgrim made a range of decorative objects in both crackled and plain colored glass. They also produced a line of satin finished items;

these were given an acid bath to degloss the surface and give a satiny feel to the glass.

Two brothers, Alessandro and Roberto Moretti, came from Italy to work at Pilgrim in the 1950s. Their introduction of glass animals, figurines, and other Venetian style items gave Pilgrim another desirable line. Since Venetian glass imports were becoming popular with American consumers, the Pilgrim Venetian glass met with success. Other Pilgrim innovations included an outstanding shade of pink (cranberry) introduced by plant manager Karel Konrad in 1968. The color was so desirable that it remains a staple today.

For a short time, many Pilgrim items also went under the name Empire, and even a separate catalog was produced. This so-called Empire glass was made at the Pilgrim factory in Ceredo using Pilgrim molds and colors, so without a label they are virtually impossible to distinguish from Pilgrim.

Through the 1970s a line called Kitchen Chemistry included canisters and jars with both utilitarian and aesthetic appeal. Other items introduced about this time were Rock Crystal Pitchers with a bumpy surface, salt and pepper shakers, paperweights, bells, plant hangers, and candle holders. In 1977-78 Pilgrim produced a series of signed studio pieces. These experimental pieces appeared only in their 1977-78 catalog.

The regular designers — Allesandro and Roberto Moretti and their brother-in-law Mario Sandon, who arrived in 1963, were the creative force at Pilgrim. Born in Italy in 1930 to a family with a glassmaking tradition dating to the seventeenth century, Roberto Moretti apprenticed at Murano glass factories as a boy. Later he attended the Instituto Technico del Vetro. He worked for Fugina delgi Angeli and executed designs by Pablo Picasso, Marc Chagall, and Jean Cocteau. Moretti came to the United States in 1958, and his work attracted national attention at the 1965-66 New York World's Fair. Roberto Moretti was described as "one of the pioneers in this country in a movement for glass-workers to design and form their individual creations." Paul N. Perrot, director of the Corning Museum of Glass in 1968, wrote:

Mr. Moretti's stylized shapes reveal a complete understanding of the fluid properties of glass and the subtle harmonies which can be achieved by understanding its inner light. His work . . . demonstrates that in skillful hands glass is a sculptural medium and that particularly happy results can be achieved when both the originator of the design and its executor are linked in one person.

His *Figure of Woman on Negative Space* was included in a major international exhibit organized by the Corning Museum of Glass with the accompanying catalog *New Glass: A Worldwide Survey.* Moretti retired in 1984 and died in 1986. His older brother Alessandro retired in 1985; Mario Sandon also retired but, on occasion, continued to bring the Murano touch to Pilgrim.

Pilgrim oval foil label.

Pilgrim arched label.

Opposite page:
Early Pilgrim label with glass blower (shown in 1951 catalog).

GLASS

...and its sculptured beauty

Massive, bold pieces of cased glass combining Blue, Topaz and Crystal, fused in stunning beauty. Made completely "off-hand," without moulds, these are the ultimate in the glass-blower's art.

999
Madonna

212
Fruit Bowl

211
Vase

208
Vase

Wine

206
Basket

202
Bowl

205
Pair of Candlesticks

201
Bowl

Cordial De

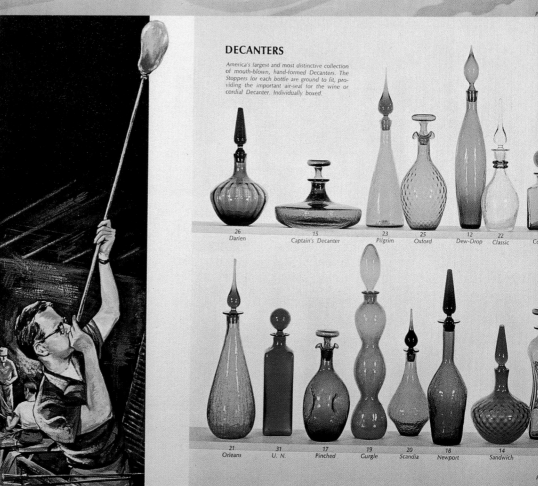

DECANTERS

America's largest and most distinctive collection of mouth-blown, hand-formed Decanters. The Stoppers for each bottle are ground to fit, providing the important air-seal for the wine or cordial Decanter. Individually boxed.

26
Darien

15
Captain's Decanter

23
Pilgrim

25
Oxford

12
Dew-Drop

22
Classic

Cor

21
Orleans

31
U. N.

17
Pinched

19
Gurgle

20
Scandia

18
Newport

14
Sandwich

Pilgrim catalog pages showing various shapes and finishes plus novelty items, such as glass animals, and an unusual line of heavy cased vessels. *Courtesy of Robert McKeand.*

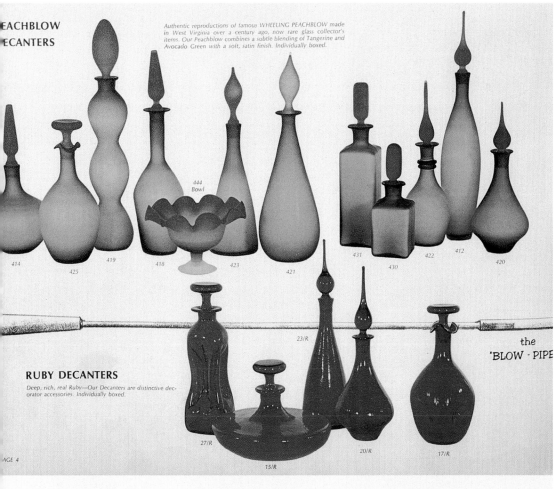

Authentic reproductions of famous WHEELING PEACHBLOW made in West Virginia over a century ago, now rare glass collector's items. Our Peachblow combines a subtle blending of Tangerine and Avocado Green with a soft, satin finish. Individually boxed.

444
Bowl

414   419   418   423   421   431   430   422   412   420
   425

23/R

the
'BLOW - PIPE

RUBY DECANTERS

Deep, rich, real Ruby—Our Decanters are distinctive decorator accessories. Individually boxed.

27/R   20/R   17/R

AGE 4

15/R

PITCHERS

Large and lovely, Pilgrim Pitchers can also be used for tall stemmed flower arrangements. Individually boxed.

American-made Pilgrim Glass continues a heritage begun in Jamestown, Virginia in 1607. Each piece is blown by mouth and formed by hand, bringing a touch of beauty to the everyday business of living.

THE PILGRIM
GLASS CORPORATION
Ceredo, West Va., U.S.A.

55   46   51   49   56   52

...the Fiery Magic of the Glassblower's Art brought to life by......

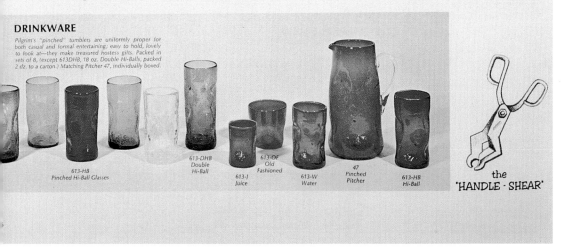

DRINKWARE

Pilgrim's "pinched" tumblers are uniformly proper for both casual and formal entertaining; easy to hold, lovely to look at—they make treasured hostess gifts. Packed in sets of 8, (except 613DHB, 18 oz. Double Hi-Balls, packed 2 dz. to a carton.) Matching Pitcher 47, individually boxed.

613-HB
Pinched Hi-Ball Glasses

613-DHB
Double
Hi-Ball

613-J
Juice

613-OF
Old
Fashioned

613-W
Water

47
Pinched
Pitcher

613-HB
Hi-Ball

the
'HANDLE · SHEAR'

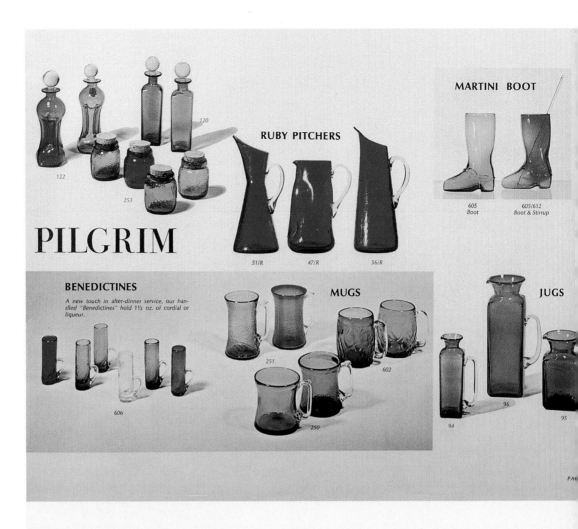

PILGRIM

RUBY PITCHERS

51/R 47/R 56/R

120

122

253

MARTINI BOOT

605
Boot

605/612
Boot & Stirrup

BENEDICTINES

A new touch in after-dinner service, our handled "Benedictines" hold 1½ oz. of cordial or liqueur.

606

MUGS

251

602

250

JUGS

94

96

95

...birds, animals and fish!

PILGRIM LARGE ANIMALS

Pilgrim is proud to present these new and exciting examples of the glassmaker's art. No two pieces are ever alike. Here is America's contribution to the 20th Century Renaissance in glass, an extension of the skills which originated in old Bohemia and Venice. Each piece is formed by the breath of the glassblower with his long blowpipe, then fashioned into unique shapes that are essentially sculpture in glass.

971
Duck

983
Marlin

906
Lucerne Fish

905
Murano Fish

981
Pigeon

975
Flamingo

973
Whimsey Cat

982
Whale

974
Whimsey Fish

976
Bear

979
Bird of Paradise

980
Owl

904
Elephant

970
Pheasant

972
Modern Bird

52

ndy snifters   cruets,   and things

68

Unusual table accents provide color and grace in the home.

09-SC

C111

C114

C110

Oil & Vinegar Cruet Sets

C112

-5C
Creamer

3

44

58-S

37

58-L

107

34

33

519

43

5

32

The Wonderful World of

..plus cats   squirrels   and dolphins

925
Siamese Cat

927
Squirrel

935
Dolphin Fish

mice   more pussy cats   wise old owls

929
Mouse

930
Pussy Cat

937
Owl

ds   prancing   horses   swans   and bambi...

926
Birds

ecting of glass animals is one of the most popu-
l hobbies. Museum collections reveal that glass
were produced in ancient times. Some collections
ck to the beginning of the Christian Era, in the
3rd Centuries—to Syria, Egypt and Palestine. The
collections are being made today at Pilgrim
n West Virginia. Each piece is completely hand
d in the ancient manner. It is one of the impor-
sfactions for the collector of Pilgrim Glass animals
piece he owns is unique, the creative expression
glass master. Each piece is made of solid glass,
by hand.

919
Prancing Horses

921
Small Swan

923
Large Swan

936
Bambi

53

Pilgrim Glass Animals

...we've even thought of snails   made satin whales   baby whal

934
Snail

964
Satin Whale

922
Small Whale

"moby dick"   frogs   and seals   kangaroos

924
Moby Dick

939
Small Frog

940
Large Frog

941
Seal

942
Kangaroo

birds again   the lowly tortoise   and the hare

963
Satin Bird

931
Small Turtle

932
Large Turtle

928
Rabbit

a horse or two   "el toro"   smokey bears   donkey

920
Horse

933
Bull

938
Smokey Bear

966
Donkey

965
Elephant

PAGE 11

-and baby elephants that are r

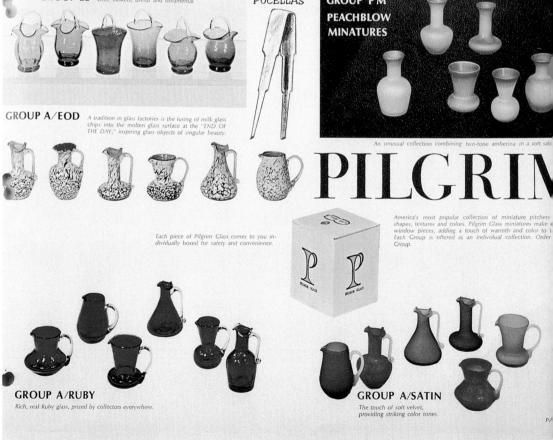

GROUP LB Little baskets, useful and ornamental

the "PUCELLAS"

GROUP P M PEACHBLOW MINATURES

GROUP A/EOD A tradition in glass factories is the fusing of milk glass chips into the molten glass surface at the "END OF THE DAY," inspiring glass objects of singular beauty.

An unusual collection combining two-tone amberina in a soft sati

PILGRIM

Each piece of Pilgrim Glass comes to you individually boxed for safety and convenience.

America's most popular collection of miniature pitchers shapes, textures and colors. Pilgrim Glass miniatures make window pieces, adding a touch of warmth and color to Each Group is offered as an individual collection. Order Group.

GROUP A/RUBY
Rich, real Ruby glass, prized by collectors everywhere.

GROUP A/SATIN
The touch of soft velvet, providing striking color tones.

P/

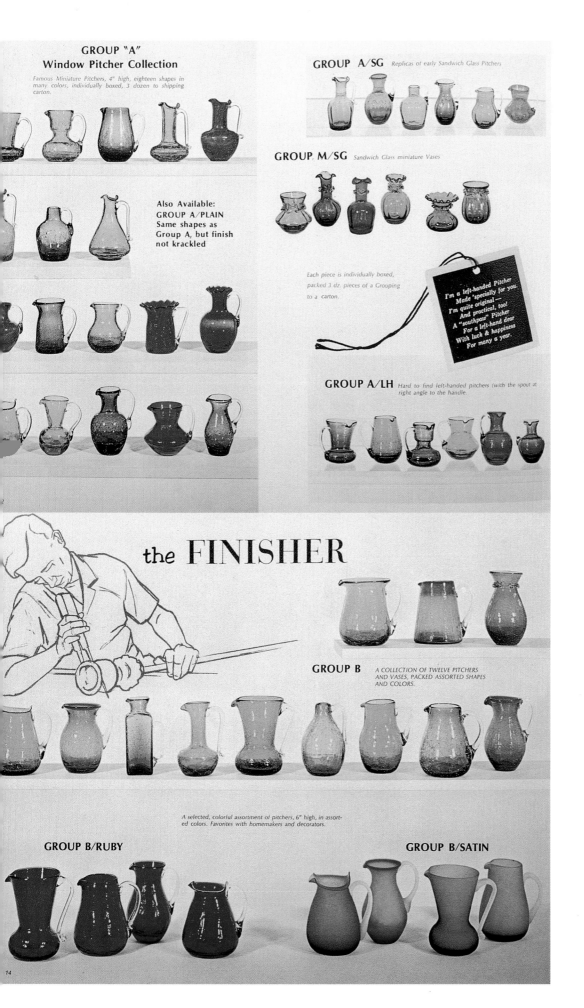

GROUP "A"
Window Pitcher Collection

Famous Miniature Pitchers, 4" high, eighteen shapes in many colors, individually boxed, 3 dozen to shipping carton.

Also Available:
GROUP A/PLAIN
Same shapes as
Group A, but finish
not krackled

GROUP A/SG Replicas of early Sandwich Glass Pitchers

GROUP M/SG Sandwich Glass miniature Vases

Each piece is individually boxed, packed 3 dz. pieces of a Grouping to a carton.

I'm a left-handed Pitcher
Made 'specially for you.
I'm quite original—
And practical, too!
A "southpaw" Pitcher
For a left-hand dear
With luck & happiness
For many a year.

GROUP A/LH *Hard to find left-handed pitchers (with the spout at right angle to the handle.*

the FINISHER

GROUP B A COLLECTION OF TWELVE PITCHERS AND VASES, PACKED ASSORTED SHAPES AND COLORS.

A selected, colorful assortment of pitchers, 6" high, in assorted colors. Favorites with homemakers and decorators.

GROUP B/RUBY

GROUP B/SATIN

14

GROUP C

A COLLECTION OF TWELVE PITCHERS AND VASES, PACKED ASSORTED SHAPES AND COLORS.

"THE FINISHER"

The most skilled of the glass craftsmen is "The Finisher" frequently referred to as the "Gaffer." It is the "Gaffer" who provides the ultimate skill to the finished piece. It is he who gently pinches, nudges, paddles, punches and shears the shape to its ultimate beauty. It is his hands which make the difference in a craft product which has never been equaled by machines. We at Pilgrim earnestly hope that you will recognize our pride not as hollow boasting, but as recognition of a product made only in an ancient manner by a company which continues the tradition of America's oldest industry . . . Glass!

A favorite group of beautiful, generous-size pitchers and vases , 7" high, in exquisite color and craftsmanship.

GROUP C/SATIN

GROUP C/RUBY

PILGRIM WEATHER GLASS

102

102/S
Teak Stand

Hand-blown replica of Weather-Forecaster used aboard the old Clipper Ships. Predicts weather changes 8 to 12 hours in advance. Gift Boxed in self-mailer, complete with black iron wall-bracket and instructions. 10½" tall.

JARS and CANISTERS

916

900

901

902

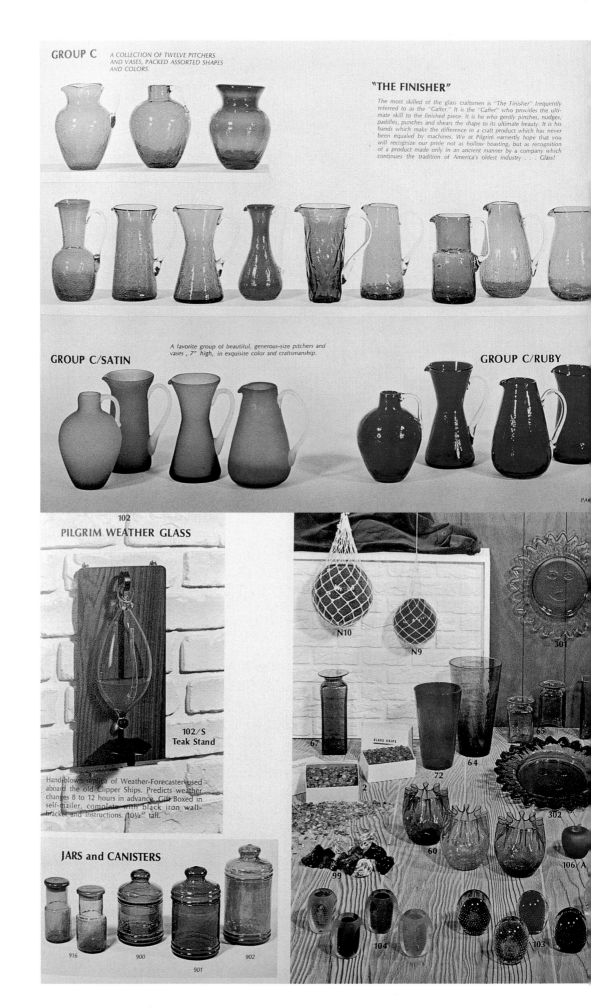

56

PILGRIM

GROUP "T" Contempo

818 *813*

814 *811*

7

ROUP "SG/R"
Ruby Sandwich Glass

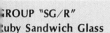

811 *817* *814* *813*

SMOKER'S CORNER

286-L *80*

79

78

285-L

284 *283*

JAMESTOWN PITCHERS

Glass was first made in Jamestown, Virginia in 1608. The shapes and textures shown on this page take their inspiration from the sturdy and rugged members of that first team of glassmakers who brought their skills from the old country and settled in the new world.

NEW !! CRANBERRY !!

Answering the strong demand from glass collectors everywhere, Pilgrim introduces a new collection of Cranberry Glass. Literally made of gold, the soft beauty of Cranberry restores to American collectors pieces which have only been available through antique dealers and private collections. Offered in limited editions, Pilgrim Glass' Cranberry will be tomorrow's antiques.

GROUP JP-Jamestown Pitchers

CRANBERRY
ASSORTMENT
NO. 1

1748 *1750* *1758*

GROUP JB/R
Ruby
Jamestown
Baskets

1759 *1762* *1764*

GROUP JB
Jamestown
Baskets

CRANBERRY
ASSORTMENT
NO. 2

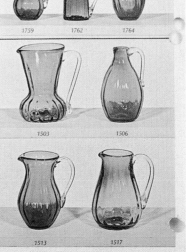

1503 *1506*

GROUP JP/R-Ruby Jamestown Pitchers

1513 *1517*

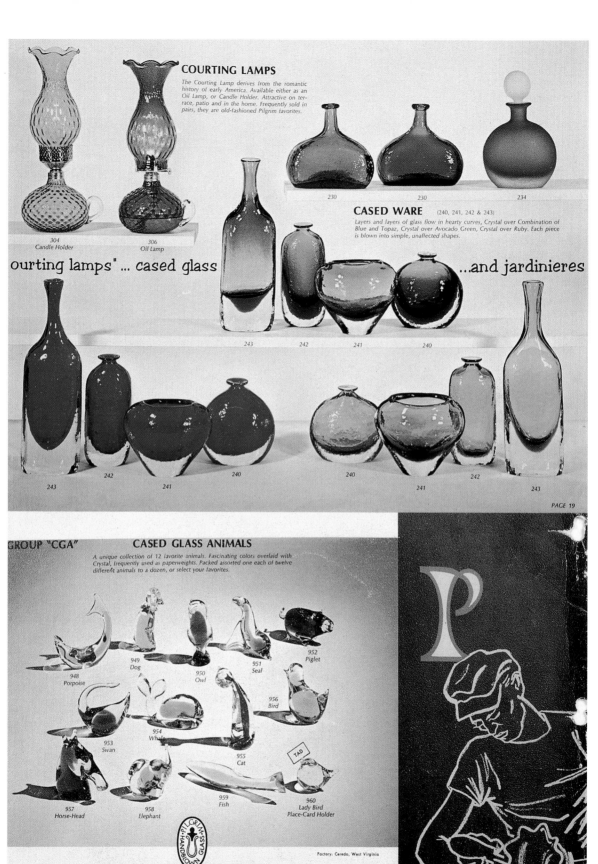

COURTING LAMPS

The Courting Lamp derives from the romantic history of early America. Available either as an Oil Lamp, or Candle Holder. Attractive on terrace, patio and in the home. Frequently sold in pairs, they are old-fashioned Pilgrim favorites.

304
Candle Holder

306
Oil Lamp

ourting lamps"... cased glass

230

230

234

CASED WARE (240, 241, 242 & 243)

Layers and layers of glass flow in hearty curves, Crystal over Combination of Blue and Topaz, Crystal over Avocado Green, Crystal over Ruby. Each piece is blown into simple, unaffected shapes.

...and jardinieres

243 **242** **241** **240**

242
243 **241**

240
241 **242** **243**

PAGE 19

GROUP "CGA"   CASED GLASS ANIMALS

A unique collection of 12 favorite animals. Fascinating colors overlaid with Crystal, frequently used as paperweights. Packed assorted one each of twelve different animals to a dozen, or select your favorites.

948
Porpoise

949
Dog

950
Owl

951
Seal

952
Piglet

956
Bird

954
Whale

953
Swan

955
Cat

957
Horse-Head

958
Elephant

959
Fish

960
Lady Bird
Place-Card Holder

Factory: Ceredo, West Virginia

Send orders to:

THE PILGRIM GLASS CORPORATION
MOONACHIE, NEW JERSEY 07074

Handy Order Form available
Price List gives full details
on sizes, shapes, finishes,
Packing Minimums and Net Prices

58

Chapter 6
Rainbow

The Rainbow Art Glass Company in Huntington, West Virginia, began in the 1940s as a glass decorating business called the Rainbow Art Company. It turned to producing its own hand blown glass in 1954 when it became the Rainbow Art Glass Company. Like other neighboring companies, they produced blown glass in vivid colors, often with a crackle finish. Rainbow made crackle through the 1970s, which was later than many of its competitors. This may account for the large number of Rainbow crackle items on the market today. In 1973 they were purchased by Viking and continued to make crackle glass until 1979. The Rainbow factory burned down in 1983, and all operations ceased.

Although many of the crackle miniatures, and even larger decanters and bottles are similar to those made at these other companies, Rainbow made a number of distinctive forms. These can often be identified by large round or elongated teardrop-shaped stoppers, and the top of the bottle neck normally has a flat collar, which also helps to differentiate Rainbow pieces. Paper labels, which identify the company may also aid in dating. In the case of Rainbow, the gold and black sun ray label is the earliest. The later silver bubble with black lettering was used on items that were sold wholesale. The same label with red lettering was used on those sold in the retail store, because they were considered "seconds."

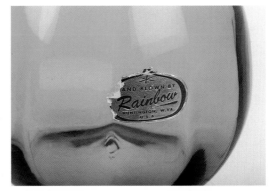

Top left: Early Rainbow label.
Bottom left: Blowing into a mold.

Top right: Rainbow red and silver label.
Bottom right: Tools of the trade.

Rainbow glass worker gathering glass.

Measuring and adjusting opening.

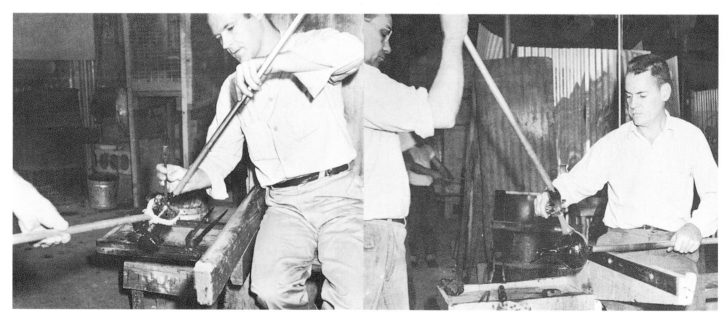

Teamwork.

Applying a handle.

The company mainstay was the crackle and plain miniature vases and pitchers that are so common in the marketplace today. Among the other more common items are copies and interpretations: Rainbow #9025 and #9055 decanter is almost identical to the Blenko model; the #512 optic pitcher resembles Anderson's early Blenko pitcher, but the Rainbow version has a narrowed neck and an added foot. Rainbow's contribution to mid-century design was neither these knock-offs nor the proliferation of ruffled miniatures. It was the occasional inspired design that Rainbow will be remembered for — like the decanter with ivy vase stopper, the tall slender bottle with long stopper, the pitcher with three-ring handle, or the decanters with oversized ball or flame stopper.

Rainbow brochure. *Courtesy of the Huntington Museum of Art.*

Rainbow catalog. In addition to the many crackle miniatures, Rainbow was known for decanters, often with large or elaborate stoppers. *Courtesy of Robert McKeand.*

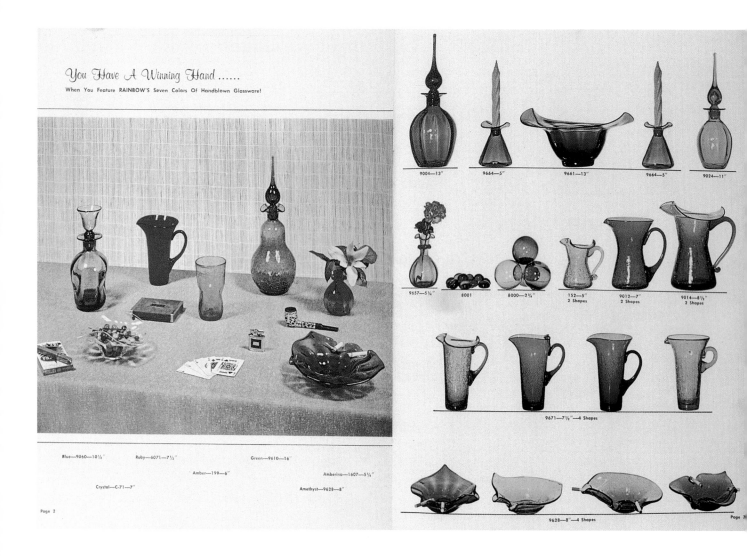

ESSEX decanter:

9055—10½"   9625—9"

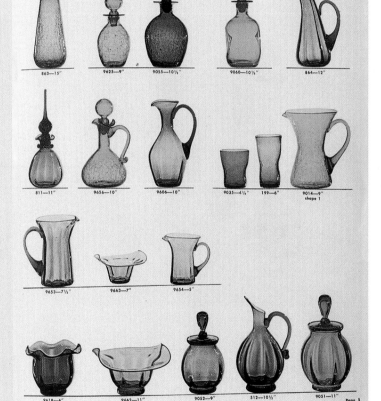

863—15"   9625—9"   9055—10½"   9060—10½"   864—12"

811—11"   9656—10"   9606—10"   9035—4¼"   199—6"   9014—9"
shape 1

9653—7½"   9663—7"   9654—5"

9618—6"   9662—11"   9052—9"   512—10½"   9051—11"

"PINCHED TUMBLER SET"—199—6"—13 oz.

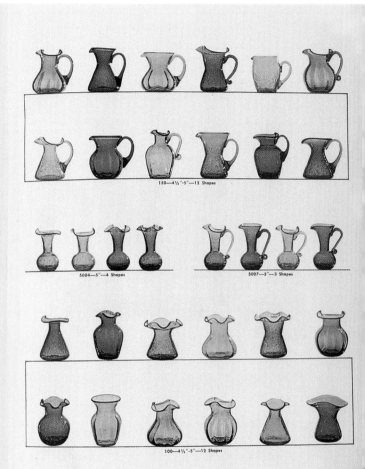

150—4½"-5"—12 Shapes

5004—5"—4 Shapes

5007—5"—3 Shapes

100—4½"-5"—12 Shapes

NEWPORT bottles:

9053—14"   9054—10"

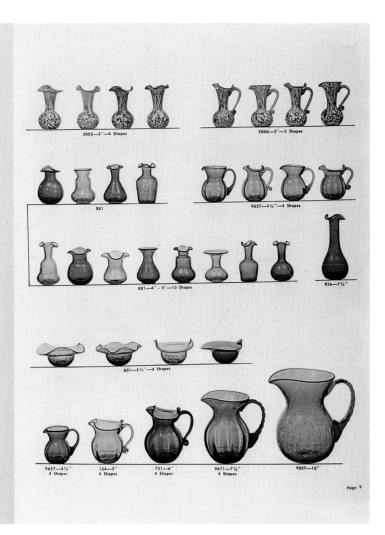

5003—5"—4 Shapes

5006—5"—3 Shapes

881

9627—4¼"—4 Shapes

881—4" - 5"—12 Shapes

836—7½"

801—5¼"—4 Shapes

9627—4¼"
4 Shapes

154—5"
4 Shapes

731—6"
4 Shapes

9611—7½"
4 Shapes

9007—10"

Hawaska

9601—23" 9602—20" 9603—17"

Hawaska

9609—10" 9608—12½" 9607—15"

Hancock

9621—12" 9620—14" 9619—16½"

Hawaska

9604—14" 9605—12" 9606—10"

Hancock

9624—6" 9623—7" 9622—8"

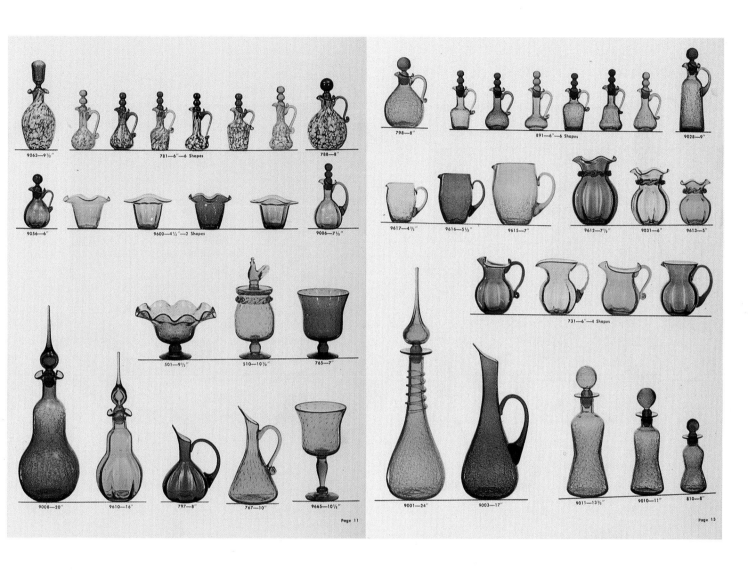

9063—9½"

781—6"—6 Shapes

788—8"

9056—6"

9600—4½"—2 Shapes

9006—7½"

501—9½"

510—10½"

765—7"

9008—20"

9610—16"

797—8"

767—10"

9665—10½"

798—8"

891—6"—6 Shapes

9028—9"

9617—4½"

9616—5½"

9615—7"

9612—7½"

9031—6"

9613—5"

731—6"—4 Shapes

9001—24"

9003—17"

9011—13½"

9010—11"

810—8"

From Fine Sand to Fine Glassware . . . .

7 Sparkling RAINBOW colors . . .

Crystal:

C-14—6"   C-29—8"   C-33—14"   C-24—6"

Amber: 9056—6"   Green: 9654—5"   Amethyst: 9665—10½"   Blue: 9619—16½"

Balls asst. col.: 8000   Clippings asst. col.: 8002
Ruby: 699

Page 18

Amberina

TAVERN pitcher: 1675—12"

DIPLOMAT decanter: 1674—17½"

ADMIRAL decanter: 1660—13"

Page 22

ruby: 611—6" — 6 Shapes   amberina: 1611—6" — 6 Shapes

1607—5¼"   1606—7½"   6062—11"   699—2¾"   6063—7"

ruby: 613   amberina: 1613   ruby: 612   amberina: 1612   6071—7½" — 2 Shapes   amberina: 1636   ruby: 636   16024—6"   6021—12"
5" — 3 Shapes   4¼"-5" — 4 Shapes   7½" — 2 Shapes   ruby: 6024   amberina: 16021

16071—7½" — 4 Shapes   6018—6"   664—15"   1697—8"   6081—10"   6012—4¼"   6011—6"   617—10"

618—20"   6010—16"   16095—12"   6094—14"   16096—10"   16030—9"   6064—5"   6061—13"   6064—5"   16059—8"
ruby: 6095   ruby: 6096

Chapter 7

Viking

The Viking Glass Company was originally called the New Martinsville Glass Manufacturing Company, which was incorporated in 1900. Like many other glass companies, New Martinsville began by making utilitarian glass and soon expanded into more ornamental items. Among their first of these were lines of colorful opalescent art glass and decorative pressed wares. Throughout the 1920s, new products were continually offered in distinctive colors.

Financial problems plagued the glass industry as much as any other in the 1930s, and the company went into receivership in 1937. A group from Connecticut purchased it and reopened as the New Martinsville Glass Co. Then, in 1944, former partner G.R. Cummings purchased all of the New Martinsville stock and changed the name to Viking Glass Company because of its reference to Scandinavia and its modern glass designs.

New Martinsville Glass can be divided into three periods : 1) 1901-07, Art and opaque glass such as Peachblow; 2) 1907-37, Pattern glass with a heavy deep pattern and brilliancy; 3) 1937-44, Crystal and some colored wares and novelty and decorative items such as candlesticks and figurines. Under the new Viking name and ownership, color became a focus. Their subsidiary, Rainbow Art Glass of Huntington (established 1939), also relied heavily of color for its identity and appeal. Both Rainbow and Viking were featured in the Corning Museum's *Glass 1959*. One of Viking's most distinctive and popular lines, called Epic, began in the early 1960s. Epic included unusual shapes that seemed to play on the drippy quality of hot glass. Long, slender-tailed birds, sometimes mounted on container lids, became

other Viking trademarks. Elmer E. Miller, who joined the company in 1923, was responsible for many of the modern designs of the 1950s and 1960s.

Viking was one of the leading West Virginia companies to contribute to American mid-century glass, but it was different from others like Blenko or Pilgrim. Rather than off-hand glass, Viking focused on fine-quality molded wares, and the forms were rarely copied by other factories. Except for a few designs closely shared with Fenton, most of Viking's plain-finish glass is exclusive to Viking and therefore very easy to identify. Among the only important crackle that Viking made were their patio lights and large heavy ashtrays. The remainder of its limited crackle production consists mostly of plain bud vases, which can easily be mistaken for the work of other companies.

Kenneth Dalzell, the fourth generation of an eighty-four-year family presidency of the Fostoria Glass Company, joined Lancaster Colony when it purchased Fostoria in 1983. Then, when Fostoria closed, Dalzell left Lancaster to head his own glass company again. He reopened Viking as Dalzell-Viking in 1987. The company continued to make high quality hand-molded glass in both crystal and vibrant colors such as ruby red and cobalt blue. In addition to decorative giftware sold at department stores and specialty shops, Dalzell-Viking made reproductions of early glass for clients such as the Smithsonian, the Metropolitan Museum of Art, Oneida, Coca-Cola, and the Heisey Collector Club. Like neighboring Blenko, Pilgrim, and Fenton, Viking was a survivor in a shrinking American hand-made glass industry until it closed in 1998.

Viking Catalog cover, 1975/6.

Viking crystal crackle in 1975/6 catalog.

Viking colored crackle in mid-1970s catalogs.

Epic

7458
13½" Vase

7557
10½" Ball Vase

7555
8" Flip Vase

7469
11" Bottle

7552
9" Pitcher

7551
9" Vase

7550
9½" Vase

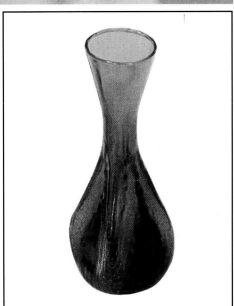

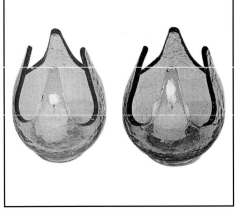

Chapter 8

Drinkware

Blenko #418-S juice tumblers in emerald green. 4-1/2" h. $15-20 each

Blenko #418-L tumbler in leaf green (shown with juice tumbler for relative size), 6" h. $15-25

Blenko tumbler in cobalt blue showing rounded bottom, usually distinguishing Blenko form other companies. $15-25

Top: Blenko tumblers in Wheat, plus unusual Blenko colors — Rosé, Charcoal, and Crystal. *Courtesy of Blenko.* $15-30 each

Bottom left: Blenko tumbler in Tangerine (amberina). *Courtesy of Blenko.* $15-25

Bottom right: Blenko #418-DOF Tangerine double old fashioned. $20-30

Blenko #600-HB highball with
Amethyst applied spiral. 6-3/4" h.
Courtesy of Blenko. $30-40

Spiral highball with other
Amethyst Blenko items.
Courtesy of Blenko.

74

Blenko #445-CT cocktail with Amethyst rosettes around the base (shown with spiral highball to show relative size). *Courtesy of Blenko.* $20-25

Left: Blenko #600-HB with spiral in Ruby and Chartreuse. *Courtesy of Blenko.* $30-40 each

Right: Blenko #445-CT with Sea Green rosettes. *Courtesy of Blenko.* $20-25

Blenko #3627 chimney highballs in Crystal. 9" h. $30-35 each

Amber tumblers with polished rim. $10-12 each

Top: Pale green tumblers with flat base, typical of Pilgrim. $15-20 each
Bottom: Pilgrim tumblers in amber. $10-15 each

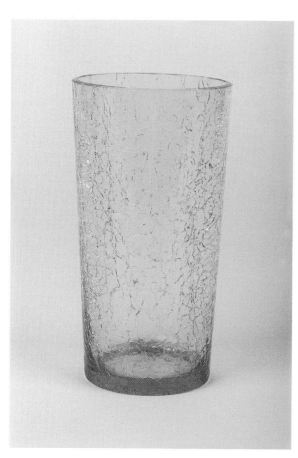

Very pale pink tumbler with polished rim. $10-15

Amber juice tumblers. $10-12 each

Blenko footed tumbler in Persian, with ball stem. *Courtesy of Blenko.* $25-35

Pilgrim #32 footed chalice in lavender, with plain stem, and showing fine "onion" crackle. 7" h. $25-35

Blenko #489 giant goblet with Crystal air twist stem and Sea Green bowl and foot, designed by Winslow Anderson in 1948. 13" h. *Courtesy of Blenko.* $70-90

Blenko #489 giant goblet with Charcoal bowl and foot. $75-95

Top left: Pilgrim #606 benedictines with orange and green bodies and crystal handles. $10-15 each

Top right: Kanawha #158 miniature 3" mugs in amberina and green. $10-15 each

Bottom left: Blenko giant mugs (3-cup capacity) in Turquoise or "Blenko Blue." $30-40 each

Bottom right: Single mug showing fairly large crackle.

Crystal mugs with tapering sides. $10-15 each

Rounded crystal mugs with Blenko Blue ribbed or reeded handles. $25-35 each

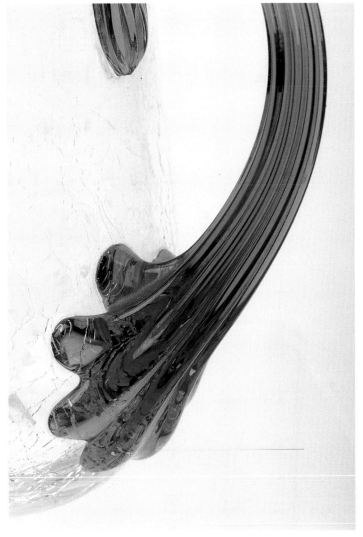

Detail of reeded handle as it attaches to the mug.

Top left: Blenko Crystal mug with reeded handle, with similar #3750-L pitcher with plain handle. *Courtesy of Blenko.* $25-35; $35-45
Bottom: Pilgrim #600-M 12-oz. beer mugs in amberina with yellow handles. $25-35 each
Top right: Detail.

Chapter 9

Miniatures

Top: Pilgrim #755 jugs are among the most commonly found miniatures. Since they are made by hand, there will be some variation among Pilgrim pieces, but sometimes this indicates that another company made the piece. 4" h. $15-20 each

Bottom left: Pilgrim miniature jug shown with Blenko #6526 14" jug to show relative size. $15-20; $75-100

Bottom right: Labeled amber Pilgrim jug flanked by blue with variation in handle and yellow. $15-20 each

Two shades of green jugs with variations in handle and body of jug. $15-20 each

Three amberina window pitchers showing variations in color, probably Hamon.

Three red jugs with angled shoulders showing variation in height, due to neck length, and in base (left is smooth). $15-20 each

Pilgrim round-shouldered jug shown with slightly taller angle-shouldered jug.

Rainbow amberina cruet/pitcher with long neck and ruffled top, shown with jug with similar body form. $15-20 each

Rainbow window pitcher in yellow and amberina. 5-3/4" h. $15-20 each

Probably Kanawha 6" window pitchers, since Kanawha was known for a molded footed base. 6" h. $10-15

Rainbow long-necked window pitchers with two different base shapes. $15-20 each

Window pitcher in a similar form with molded spiral around neck. 5-5/8" h. $15-20

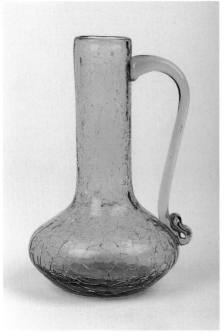

Pilgrim #751 long-necked jug (no pouring spout). 4-1/2" h. $15-20

Pilgrim #751 jug in red. *Courtesy of Sheila Randel.* $15-20

Rainbow 5" window pitchers in amberina and amber. $15-20; $10-15

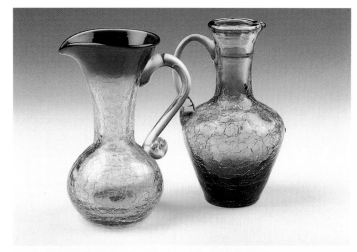

Pilgrim #767 window pitchers in amberina. 4-1/2" h. $15-20 each

Brown window pitcher with sloping shoulders with Pilgrim #767 showing opposite body form. $10-15; $15-20

Green crackle window pitchers, probably Hamon and Pilgrim (right). 5" h. $15-20 each

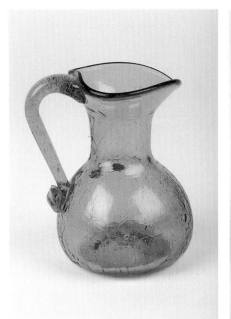

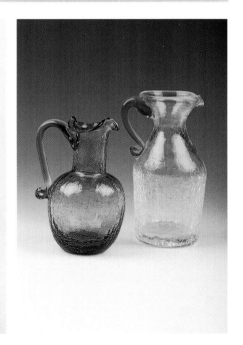

Top left: Probably Rainbow window pitcher, similar to Pilgrim but without tapered bottom. 4-3/4" h. $10-15

Top right: Pilgrim #757 window pitchers. 3-1/2" h. $10-20 each

Bottom left: Pilgrim #748 green and Rainbow #612 cobalt window pitcher. 3-5/8" h. and 4-1/4" h. $10-20 each

Bottom right: Pilgrim window pitchers with variation in body shape and handle, showing same or contrasting color. 4-1/2" h. and 5" h. $15-20 each

Two variations of Kanawha window pitchers. 4-1/4" h. and 4-3/4" h. $10-20 each

Red window pitchers with yellow handles, left to right, probably Kanawha, Pilgrim, and Rainbow. $15-20 each

Turquoise window pitchers with similar forms, possibly Rainbow. 4-1/2" h. and 3-1/2" h. $15-20 each

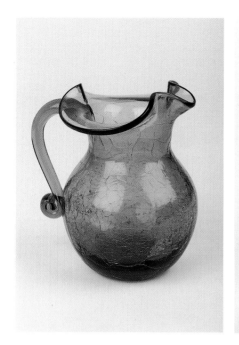

Top left: Rainbow light amethyst 5" window pitcher. *Courtesy of the Huntington Museum of Art.* $15-20

Top right: Rainbow deep amethyst and Kanawha yellow 5" window pitchers. $15-20 each

Bottom left: Rainbow #201 window pitchers with pinched waists. 3-1/2" h. $10-15 each

Bottom right: Amberina Pilgrim/Empire window pitcher with crystal handle. $15-20

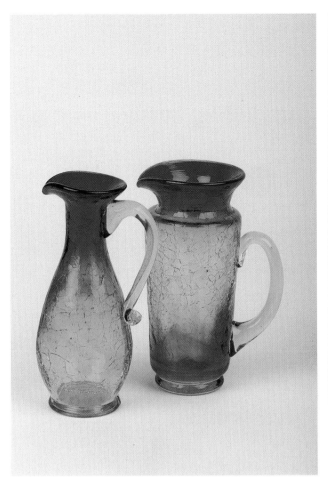

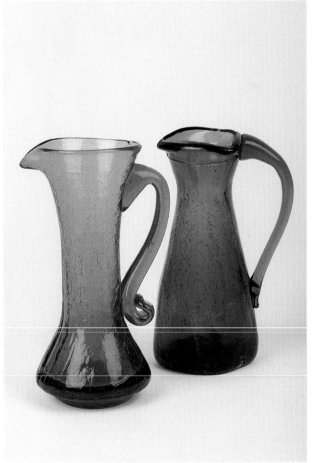

Top left: Kanawha amberina window pitchers in different shapes, both with typical Kanawha molded foot. 5-1/2" h. and 5-1/4" h. $10-15 each

Top right: Kanawha 5-1/2" window pitchers in green (with label) and lighter amberina. $10-15 each

Bottom right: Kanawha 5-1/2" window pitcher with unidentified 5-1/4" window pitcher. $10-15 each

Kanawha 3" window pitcher with unidentified window pitcher in deeper shade of lime green. $10-15 each

Rainbow #9716 ruby window pitcher with unidentified similar form in green. 3-1/4" h. and 3-5/8" h. $10-15 each

Pilgrim cylindrical window pitchers. 3" to 4" h. $10-15 each

Hamon, Rainbow, and Pilgrim #762 window pitchers. 3-1/2" h., 4" h., and 4-1/2" h. $10-15 each

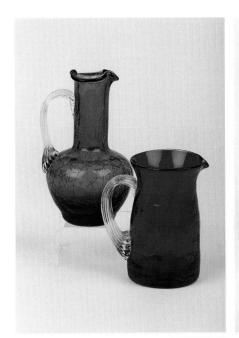

Top left: Pilgrim window pitchers: long-necked blue with no-neck red window pitcher, both with crystal reeded handle. $15-20 each

Center left: Pilgrim #761 blue window pitcher with angular crystal handle. 3-3/4" h. $15-20

Top right: Amberina 5" window pitchers with conical form and ruffled top. $15-20 each

Center right: Pilgrim #756 window pitchers in more squat conical form with ruffled top. 4-3/4" h. $15-20 each

Bottom: Pilgrim #756 window pitcher with Rainbow window vase using similar shape. $15-20 each

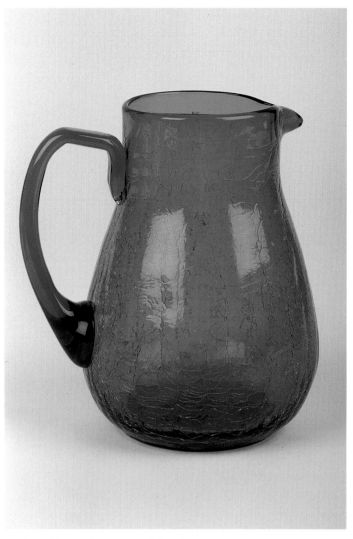

Probably Pilgrim 5-1/2" pitcher. $25-35

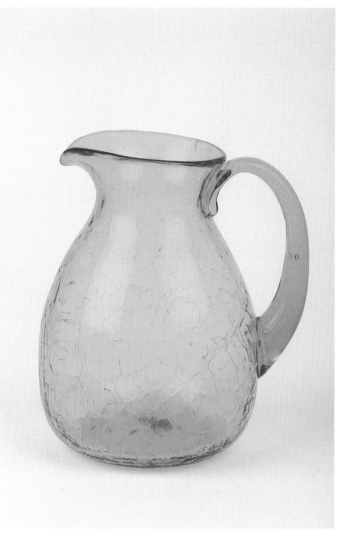

Similar pitcher in yellow. *Courtesy of the Huntington Museum of Art.* $25-35

Pilgrim Group A #759 amber and tangerine pitchers, with Group B #513 in blue. 3-3/4" h. and 4-3/4" h. $10-15; $15-20

Rainbow chartreuse and Pilgrim gold window pitchers. 5" h. and 5-3/4" h. $15-20; $25-35

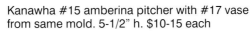
Kanawha #15 amberina pitcher with #17 vase from same mold. 5-1/2" h. $10-15 each

Pilgrim Group A #757 amethyst window pitcher, with grayish amethyst window vase, probably by Hamon. 3-1/2" h. and 5-1/4" h. $15-20 each

Example of same 5" mold used for window pitcher and vase. $10-15 each

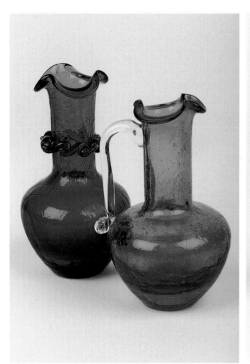

Pilgrim forms: left, green with applied scroll decoration; right, red with crystal handle. 4-1/2" h. $15-20 each

Cobalt blue cylindrical vase with applied scrolls, with Pilgrim #471 vase with same decoration. 5-1/2" h. and 4-1/2" h. $15-20 each

Green window vase with applied scrolls, probably Hamon. *Courtesy of the Huntington Museum of Art.* $15-20

Green window pitcher and yellow Kanawha vase, both with applied scrolls and ruffled top. 3-1/2" h. $10-15 each

Detail.

Blenko Olive Green, Sea Green, and Turquoise
4-1/2" miniature vases. $15-20 each

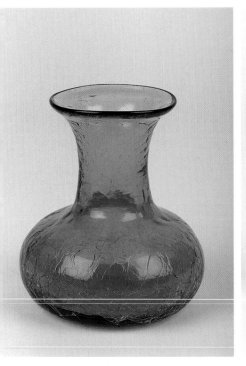

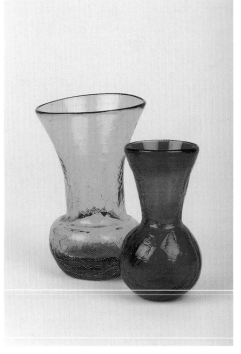

Blenko Sea Green 4-1/2" miniature,
though Bischoff made the same form.
$15-20

Possibly Blenko red and green miniature
vases. 4" h. and 3-1/2" h. $10-15 each

Rainbow chartreuse window vase
shown with (Blenko) in same shape. 4-
3/4" h. and 4" h. $10-15 each

Blenko CM-6 miniature vases in Turquoise and Honey.
4-3/4" h. and 5" h. $15-20 each

Blenko miniature #3615-G in Sea Green, shown with
CM-7 (left) in same color. 4-5/8" h. $15-20 each

Blenko Olive Green CM-5 and CM-3
miniatures. $15-20 each

Blenko Sea Green CM-7 miniature vase
with similar turquoise vase. 4-1/2" h. and
4" h. $15-20; $10-15

Blenko miniature vases in Wheat and
Olive Green. 4-5/8" h. $15-20 each

Rainbow window vases with ruffled tops in two shades of green. 5" h. to 5-3/8" h. $15-20 each

Rainbow #100 in turquoise with taller version in amber. $15-20 each

Slightly taller copy of Blenko 3615-G in light blue, with ground rim. 5-1/4" h. $10-15

Kanawha #123 vase with molded foot. 3" h. $7-10

Probably Pilgrim window vase in light green with applied spiral. $15-20

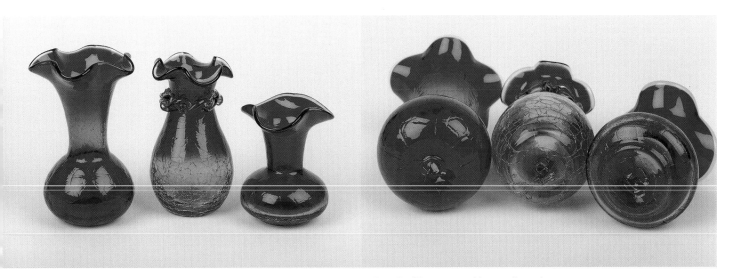

Group of Rainbow Amberina vases with ruffled tops. 4" h. to 5-1/2" h. $15-20 each

Detail of bottoms with pontil mark.

Chapter 10

Handles

Top left: Blenko #976, large honey crackle pitcher, designed by Winslow Anderson c. 1950. 19-1/2" h. $75-100

Top right: Two Blenko #976 pitchers showing variation due to their large size and to being hand blown. $75-100 each

Bottom left: Kanawha #85 amberina pitcher with elongated spout, a commonly seen example with variation in height, averaging 14". $35-45 each

Bottom right: Kanawha pitchers with several variations: one with bent spout, different handles, and amberina coloration. $35-45 each

Large red cylindrical pitcher with crystal handle, by Bischoff; shown with Pilgrim benedictines in same form to show relative size. 13-1/2" h. $70-90

Window pitcher with Kanawha pitcher, both with yellow handle. 4" h. and 8" h. $10-15; $25-35

Pitchers with flared openings: Rainbow ruby "Long John," similar form in amber, and Blenko #6030-S in Persian designed by Wayne Husted (with sandblasted signature only used in 1959/60). 12 h., 13 h., and 10-1/2" h. $50-80 each

Rainbow Long John pitcher with miniature in similar shape. 12" h. and 3-3/4" h. $70-80; $15-20

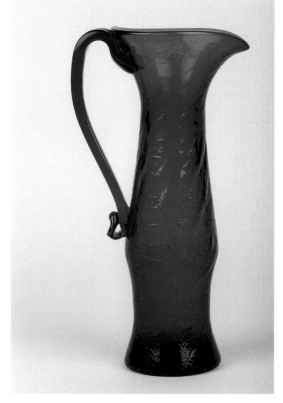

Blenko #6030-S.

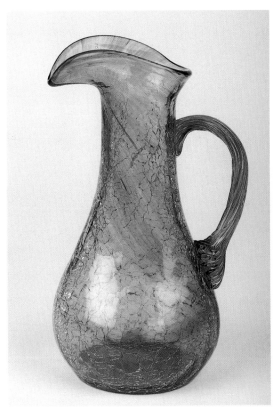

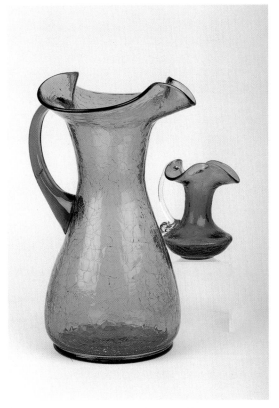

Rainbow green pitcher with extended spout.
8-1/2" h. $35-45

Kanawha 11" lime green pitcher with wavy
opening, shown with miniature with similar form.
$40-50; $15-20

Blenko #569 Tangerine pitcher with flat handle,
designed by Wayne Husted and introduced in
1956. 13" h. $50-70

Blenko #569 showing flat handle, with 5-1/2"
pitcher in similar shape. $50-70; $15-20

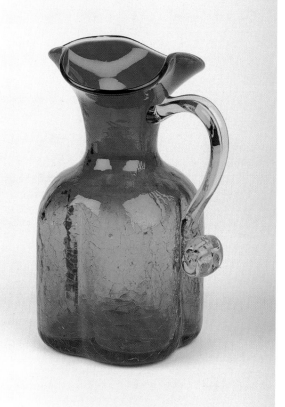

Top: Rainbow amberina and purple pitchers with two bulbous sections. 5-3/4" h. and 7-1/2" h. $25-35; $35-45

Bottom: Detail of handles.

Top: Amberina four-lobed pitcher with yellow handle, possibly Rainbow. 8" h. $30-40

Bottom: Amberina pitcher, possibly Rainbow, with flattened rounded form that appears round in this view. 10-1/4" h. $50-60

Amberina pitchers in a variety of shapes and sizes. 3-1/4" h. to 7-1/2" h. $15-25 each

Bulbous bottom and flaring top: left, Pilgrim pitcher; center, Rainbow vase; right, Blenko miniature. 4" h. to 7" h. $15-30 each

Rainbow pitcher with contrasting handle, with vase of same form but without handle. 5-1/2" h. $15-25 each

Pilgrim Group B #513 blue, Group C amber, Group A #759
amber, and Group C #685 in light blue. 3-5/8" h. to 6-1/8" h.
$15-20 small; $25-35 larger

Pilgrim Group C #685 green pitcher
with same shape Pilgrim Group A #759.
5-5/8" h. and 3-3/4" h. $25-35; $15-20

Rainbow amberina pitcher. 5-3/8"
h. $25-35

Blenko #3750-L Sea Green pitcher.
5-1/2" h. $30-40

Top left: Blenko C60F miniature pitcher in Jonquil, in same shape as 3750. 3-1/2" h. $15-25

Top right: Blenko #3750-L Tangerine pitchers. *Courtesy of the Huntington Museum of Art.* $30-40 each

Right: Blenko #939 14" pitcher with elongated spout, designed by Winslow Anderson c. 1950, shown with Tangerine 3750-L. $60-70

Molded "faux crackle" texture on blown 8" pitcher, signed Chet Cole. $40-50

Detail.

Blenko #6714 designed by Joel Myers and introduced in 1967, in Wheat with pinched spout and dented sides. 9" h. $40-50

Amber pitchers with pinched spouts: Pilgrim with graduated color, shown with Blenko 6714 dented. 10-1/2" h. $35-45

Amber pitcher with pinched spout, similar to a Pilgrim model, but with molded foot, indicative of Kanawha. 8"h. $30-35

Blenko #5424 amber jug, designed by Wayne
Husted and introduced in 1954. 12" h. $70-90

Top: Group of crystal items with applied handles: all Blenko with Blenko Blue, except for pitcher in front with lighter shade of turquoise.
Bottom left: Blenko #417, 8" Crystal jug with Turquoise handle and #6526, 14" Honey jug, designed by Joel Myers and introduced in 1965. $35-45; $75-100
Bottom right: Rainbow #327, 6" red jug. $25-35

Chapter 11

Decanters

Blenko decanters in Blenko Blue and
Olive Green with applied spiral rope
(with plain bottle-vase) designed by Joel
Myers. *Courtesy of Blenko*

Opposite page:
Top left: Blenko #6838 decanter designed by Myers and introduced in 1968, in Blenko Blue with applied Olive Green spiral. 16" h. *Courtesy of Blenko*. $125-150

Top right: Blenko #6836 footed decanter designed by Myers and introduced in 1968, in Olive Green with applied Blenko Blue spiral. 13-3/4" h. *Courtesy of Blenko*. $100-125

Bottom left: Blenko #445, introduced in 1944, in crystal with applied Sea Green rosettes on the base and on top of the large stopper. 12" h. $100-150

Bottom right: Detail of stopper.

Rainbow # 933 and #315 amberina decanters with large flame stoppers. 13-1/2 h. and 16-1/2" h. $50-70; $75-100

Blenko #657-M Tangerine decanter with elongated neck and cylindrical stopper, designed by Joel Myers and introduced in 1965. 14" h. $70-90

Blenko #920-M Tangerine decanters designed by Winslow Anderson, c. 1950, one of the most popular and most copied of the Blenko designs. The plain finish example on the left with the wider stopper might be by another company. 16-1/2" h. $60-80 each

Blenko #920 in Ruby with a less common crackle stopper. *Courtesy of Blenko.* $70-90

Opposite page: Blenko #657-S Olive Green (more chartreuse) decanter with medium Tangerine to show relative size. 12" h. $60-80

Blenko #6122-S Tangerine decanter, designed by Wayne Husted and introduced in 1961, with wide flat base, long neck, and extra long flame stopper (fits loosely in neck, because neither stopper or neck is ground like the other styles of Blenko stoppers). 16-1/2" h. $75-100

Blenko #627-L Honey decanter, designed by Husted and introduced in 1962, with elongated neck and flame stopper. 18" h. $75-100

Top left: Pilgrim bent decanter, a copy of Anderson's award-winning design for Blenko, c. 1950. The handle of the original is placed slightly higher, and the mushroom stopper is smaller. 14" h. $70-90 (original is more valuable)

Top right: Kanawha #248 molded decanter with fruit design on lower portion and unusual stopper in the shape of a tropical plant; with Blenko #6123 Tangerine bottle, designed by Husted (missing stopper). Decanter, 15-1/2" h. $70-90

Right: Detail of stopper.

Top left: Turquoise decanter in unusual lobed form, with crystal stopper. 12-1/2" h. $60-70
Top right: Blenko #475 Crystal decanter with applied Blenko Blue rings and solid conical stopper (shown with Sea Green, missing stopper). 15" h. $100-150
Bottom left: Blenko #6516 Olive Green decanter with long neck and complex stopper, deigned by Myers and introduced in 1965. 14-1/2" h. $75-100
Bottom right: Blenko #6516 Tangerine decanters showing variation in stoppers. $75-100 each

Blenko #6629 Honey decanter, designed by Myers and introduced in 1966, with very wide flat base and long neck. 12-5/8" h. $75-100

Pilgrim #20 decanter with low sloping shoulders and angled tapered bottom. 14-1/2" h. $60-80

Rainbow #9060 rounded decanter with dents, flat collar, and flamboyant flame stopper. 15" h. $100-125

Rainbow amberina cylindrical
bottle with large round stopper.
8-1/2" h. $40-60

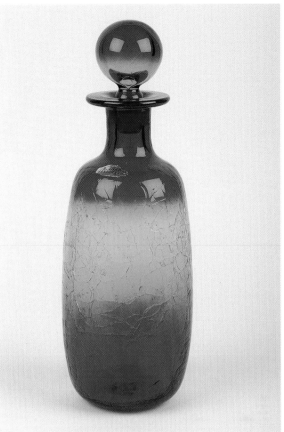

Top left: Blenko #7412 Tangerine decanter, with atypical flat collar, designed by John Nickerson and introduced in 1974. 11" h. $70-90

Top right: Blenko #7323 Tangerine decanter with flat collar, designed by John Nickerson and introduced in 1973. 13" h. $75-100

Bottom left: Blenko #654 Blenko Blue decanter, designed by Joel Myers and introduced in 1965, with solid ball stopper (less common than the hollow ball). 12" h. $70-90

Bottom right: Detail of stopper with trapped air bubble.

Blenko #649 Olive Green (more like chartreuse) decanter, designed by Myers and introduced in 1964, with stopper as up-side-down image of bottle shape (shown with 636 for comparison). 13-1/2" h. $75-100

Blenko #636 Jonquil decanter, designed by Wayne Husted and introduced in 1963, with hollow ball stopper. 11" h. $70-90

Unusual Rainbow hot pink stained decanter with
fantastic stopper in the form of a pinched ivy vase, and
applied crystal rings. 13" h. $200-250

Shown with stopper removed.

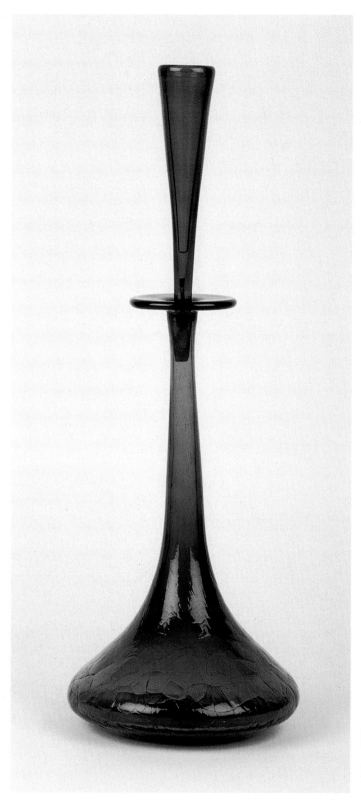

Blenko #6027 Amethyst decanter, designed by Husted and introduced in 1960, with extremely narrow neck and open stopper in the shape of a shot glass. 17" h. *Courtesy of Myra Fortlage.* $125-150

Blenko #6422 Olive Green bottle-vase, designed by Myers and introduced in 1964, (shown with variation of shot-glass stopper from 6027 decanter). Bottle, 17" h. $100-125

Bischoff #478 turquoise decanter
with dented body and arched
neck, with crystal teardrop
stopper. 13" h. $60-70

Blenko #49 Jonquil pinched decanter, one of the most common of
the early designs, with dented sides
and mushroom or button stopper. 10-
1/2" h. $50-60

Blenko ruby with Pilgrim blue pinched decanter.
Pilgrim crackle is very fine, and the neck is
slightly longer than Blenko.

Rainbow #9761
turquoise gurgle bottle
with flat collar and
large bubble stopper.
8-1/2" h. $50-60

Rainbow gurgle bottles
with stoppers removed to
show similarity to the
Rainbow pitcher.

Blenko #37 in ruby, one of the most common early designs and widely copied by others, shown with crackle stopper. 13-1/2" h. $50-60

More color choices for #37.

Kanawha footed version with
Blenko #37.

Vases

Turquoise vase with long, narrow neck and applied crystal scrolling, with identical form used as a decanter with ground area inside neck to receive the stopper. 6-1/2" h. $25-35 ($40-50 with stopper)

Cobalt blue bud vase with foot and ruffled top. 8" h. $15-25

Rainbow #836 amberina vase with bulbous bottom, long neck, and ruffled top. 7" h. $25-35

Rainbow #836 vases in various colors, with ruffled tops. 7" h. to 7-1/2" h. $25-35 each

Top: Rainbow amber cylindrical vase with ruffled top. 9-1/2" h. $40-50

Bottom: Probably Pilgrim turquoise vase with squat bulbous bottom, wide flared neck, and ruffled top. 5-1/4" h. $25-35

Top: Bischoff #512 ruby vase in shape of a top hat with curled rim. 6" h. $25-35

Bottom: Old Hickory Glass, by Central Glass Co. of Spiro, Oklahoma, with angled shoulders and tightly ruffled top. 9" h. $25-35

Blenko #6833-LT Lemon with Tangerine spiral trim, designed by Myers and introduced in 1968 (also made into a decanter with ground neck and stopper). 10-1/4" h. $60-80

Detail of spiral.

Blenko #404-S Jonquil fluted vase (shown with medium vase to show relative size). 9" h. $30-40

Blenko #404-M Amethyst fluted vase. 11-1/2" h. $50-60

Blenko #404-S in Rosé, a color only made in the early 1960s. 9" h. *Courtesy of Blenko.* $40-50

Group of early Blenko Crystal pieces with
applied decoration. *Courtesy of Blenko.*

Blenko #479 Crystal vase with scalloped top, applied Sea Green foot and rosettes. 9-1/2" h. *Courtesy of Blenko.* $75-100

Detail of rosette.

Photo from 1940s Blenko catalog showing items with applied decorations. *Courtesy of Blenko.*

366LL

423L   423S

366ML   366SL   422L   422M   422S

C445HB   C445OF   C445CT   33L   C445LB

C445FB   C445IB   C445SB

C445D   C439LL   C439SL   C479   C445P

Blenko Crystal beaker vase with applied blobs. *Courtesy of Blenko.* $50-60

Blenko vases with applied leaves and rosettes.

Blenko #366-SL beaker vase in
Crystal with applied green leaves. 7"
h. $50-60

Detail of leaf.

Blenko #366-SL beaker vase in Blenko
Blue with matching leaves. $60-80

138

Opposite page:
Top left: Blenko #439-SL slightly fluted Crystal vase with applied Blenko Blue rosettes. 7-1/2" h. $60-80

Top right: Detail of rosettes.

Bottom: Blenko #439 vases in crystal crackle: large with applied Sky Blue trim, smaller with applied Blenko Blue and Sea Green trim. 7-1/2" h. and 13" h. $60-80; $125-175

Blenko beaker vases with leaf and "ear" decoration.

Blenko #336-SL in Tangerine with Tangerine leaves, a more desirable color than the more common Crystal. *Courtesy of the Huntington Museum of Art.* $60-80

Blenko #473 Crystal vase with applied Blenko Blue "ears" or "wings." 8" h. $70-90

Opposite page:
Top: Blenko #366-ML medium Crystal vase with Wheat leaves, and #473 Crystal vase with applied Sea Green "ears." 10" h. and 8" h. $70-90 each

Bottom: Blenko #366-LL large leaf vase in Crystal with Sea Green leaves, shown with the three other sizes of beaker vases. 13" h. $125-150

Blenko #5519-S Blenko Blue cylindrical vase with tapered waist, designed by Husted and introduced in 1955, shown with miniature of same form. 9" h. $35-45

Blenko #7215 ruby vase with molded ring around the lower half, designed by Nickerson and introduced in 1972. 8-1/2" h. $40-50

Detail.

Pilgrim #673 amber vase with pinched waist and applied spiral, with #503 long-necked bottle-vase with applied spiral. 7-1/2" h. and 6-3/4" h. $35-45; $20-30

Detail.

Opposite page: Blenko #6815-TO and #6815-OT 9"- vases designed by Myers and introduced in 1968, in Turquoise (Blenko Blue) with applied Olive Green snake and in Olive Green with Turquoise. $70-90 each

Crystal bud vase. 6-3/4" h. $15-25

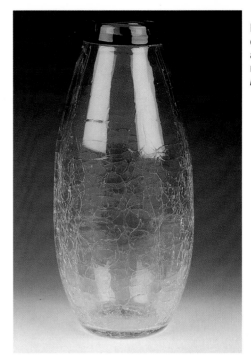

Blenko Crystal crackle with applied two-tone rim. *Courtesy of Blenko.*

Blenko #713 Olive Green vase; Pilgrim tall brown bottle-vase; amethyst vase similar to Blenko design. 10" h., 15" h., and 9" h. $25-35; 50-60; 20-30

Blenko #6311-L Olive green 16" vase with Blenko #713 similar 10" version, shown with small vase to show relative size. $60-70; 30-40; 15-20

Blenko #713 in red, designed by Myers and introduced in 1971. 10-1/4" h. $35-45

Large Blenko pear-shaped vase designed by Anderson.
Courtesy of Winslow Anderson. $70-90

Top: Amber and brown vases. 8-5/8" h. and 9" h. $30-40 each

Bottom: Blenko #6424 Blenko Blue candle holder or vase, designed by Myers and introduced in 1964, one of his most popular designs. 5-1/4" h. $25-35

Blenko #6424 in Blenko Blue, Tangerine, and
Olive Green. $25-35 each

Although crackle is usually associated more with the 1950s-1970s, it is still being made. These Blenko #9812 Kiwi (similar to Olive Green) mushroom vases were designed by Matt Carter and introduced in 1998. 8-1/4" h. $50-60 each

Blenko #6422 Olive Green vase with narrow neck and flat collar, designed by Myers and introduced in 1964, shown with early Blenko miniature in similar form. 17" h. $100-125; $20-25

Blenko #6937 Blenko Blue tall bottle-vase,
designed by Myers and introduced in 1969.
22-1/4" h. $100-120

Kanawha #38 and similar bottle-vase in amberina with stretched neck,
irregular opening, and footed base. 16-18" h. $40-60

Blenko #7223 Blenko Blue tall bottle-vase with irregular opening, designed by Nickerson and introduced in 1972 (shown with #64-B to show relative size). 25" h. $100-120

Blenko #6427 Ruby bottle-vase, designed by Myers, with heavy "paperweight" base, straight sides, and irregular opening (as well as variable height), shown with his small version for comparison. 25-1/2" h. $125-175

Opposite page: Blenko #64-B bottle vases, designed by Myers and introduced in 1964. 10" h. $25-35 each

Blenko #64-B bottle vases in additional colors,
showing variation in height. $25-35 each

Group of ivy bowls.

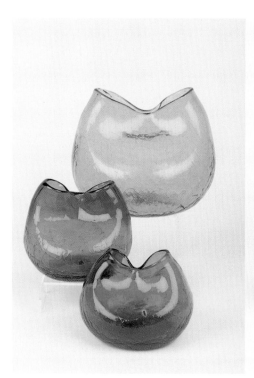

Blenko #39 ivy vases in small and large sizes. $15-35 each

Two sizes and shades of green ivy vases. $15-35 each

Ruby Blenko ivy vase with more elongated Bischoff versions. $15-35 each

Blenko 3" miniature ivy vases. $15-20 each

Bischoff ivy vases. $15-20 each

Blenko small and large ivy vases. $15-35 each

Group of pinched or dented vases.

Pilgrim #60 free form dented vase, after
Anderson's larger dented vase for Blenko.
9-1/2" h. $50-60

Rainbow #9847 early dented 9" bud
vase in olive green. $25-35

Blenko #533 four-sided bud vase,
designed by Anderson and introduced in 1953. 7" h. $25-35

Variation of ivy vase, with narrow top. $15-20

Rainbow #6021 vase with pinched ivy top portion and rounded bottom. 5" h. $15-20

Pilgrim #71 "Continental" crimped vase with ten crimps (the Blenko version has eight). 6" h., 7" d. $60-80

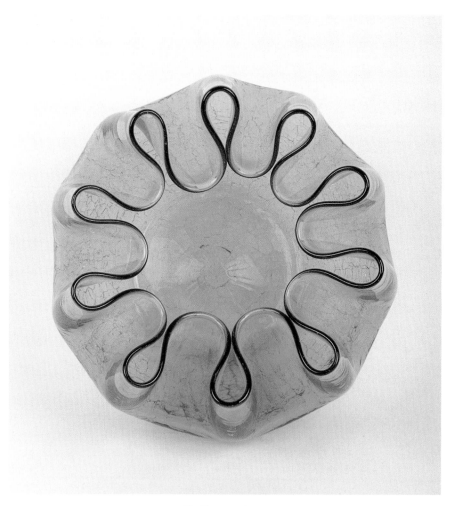

Bird's-eye view.

Viking patio lights in olive green and
ruby. $25-35 each

Ruby patio light.

Patio lights with reflection.

Chapter 13

Bowls

Viking #27 heavy green ashtrays in common small size and unusual large version. 9-1/2" d. and 7-1/2" d. $45-55; $25-35 each

Viking 7-1/2"ashtrays in amber.
$25-35 each

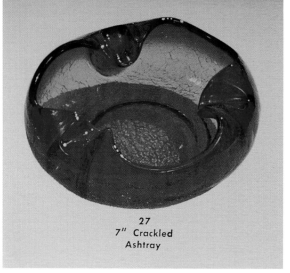

27
7" Crackled
Ashtray

Top: Viking ashtrays in orange and blue, more desirable colors. $35-45

Bottom left: Bird's-eye view.

Bottom right: Orange ashtray in 1971 Viking catalog.

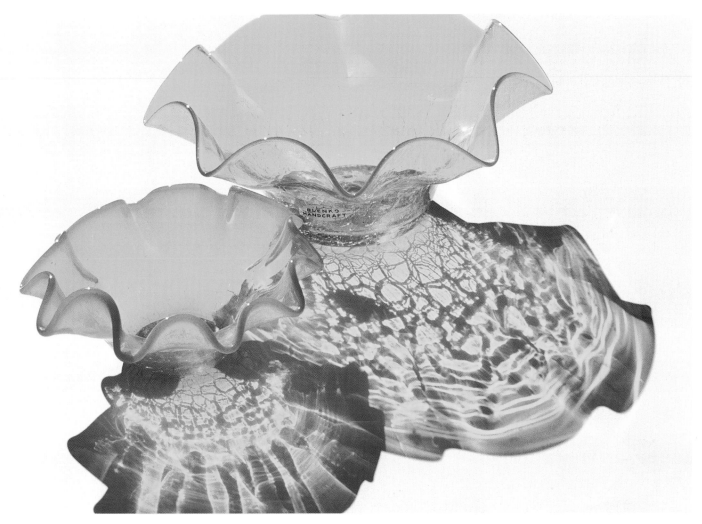

Ruffled bowl in marigold with orange opalescent edge; with
Blenko Jonquil ruffled bowl. 6" d. and 8" d. $25-35 each

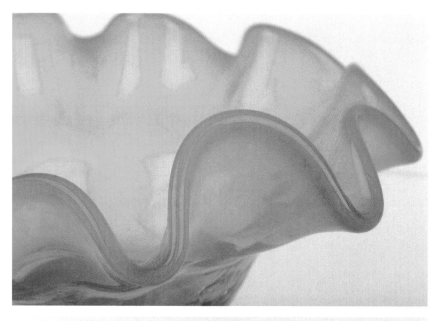

Edge detail.

Marigold nappy,
shown with ruffled
bowl in same color.
5" d. $25-35

Blenko Jonquil ruffled bowl, Kanawha turquoise ruffled bowl, and 10-1/2" diameter charcoal bowl with foot. $20-25; $15-20; $45-55

Large charcoal ruffled bowl with foot, probably either Bischoff or Kanawha. 10-1/2" d. $45-55

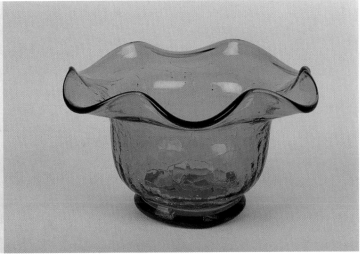

Pilgrim #58-S small ruffled bowl and Kanawha #154 ruffled bowl with foot. $15-20 each

Kanawha ruffled bowl in turquoise. *Courtesy of Myra Fortlage.* $15-20

Pilgrim #109S sugar
bowl (shown with
beaker vase). $15-20

Blenko miniature bowl in amethyst, shown with vase in same color.
Courtesy of Blenko. $15-20; 25-35

Blenko Jonquil miniature bowl with rigaree
(applied scroll) top. 2-5/8" h. $15-20

Chapter 14

Figural

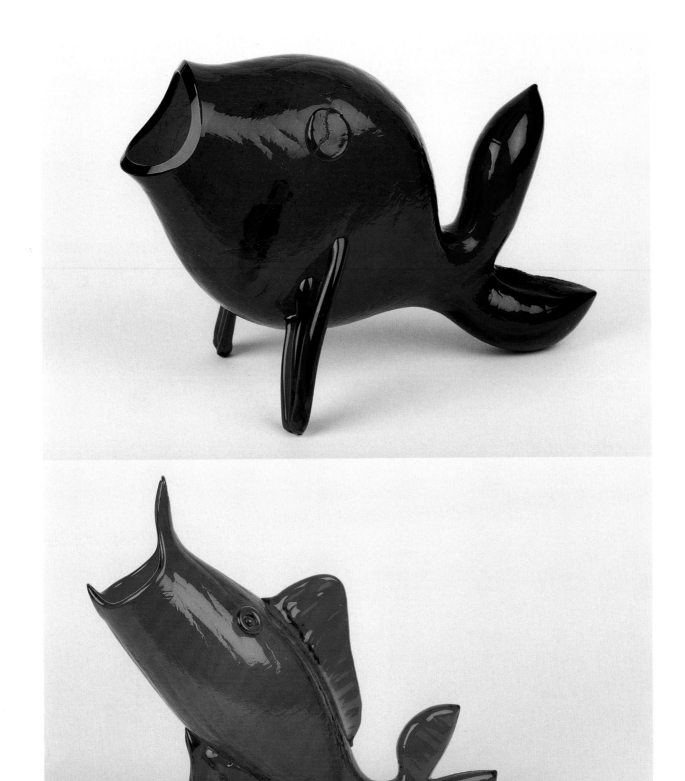

Top: Blenko #5433 cobalt fish, designed by Husted as a variation of the popular longer and narrower fish Anderson had designed a few years earlier. 10" h. x 12-1/2" l. $100-125
Bottom: Rainbow 12" orange fish with top fin and tail similar to the Blenko version. $70-90

Opposite page: Rainbow orange and Blenko Blue fish.

Top: Wine bottle in the shape of a fish with green eyes, label: "Orvieto Wine 1967 Italy." 15-1/2" l. $30-40
Bottom: Two Italian fish bottles showing variations in fin, eye placement, etc. $30-40 each

Blenko Crystal cowboy hat with applied Sea Green rosettes. *Courtesy of the Huntington Museum of Art.* $40-50

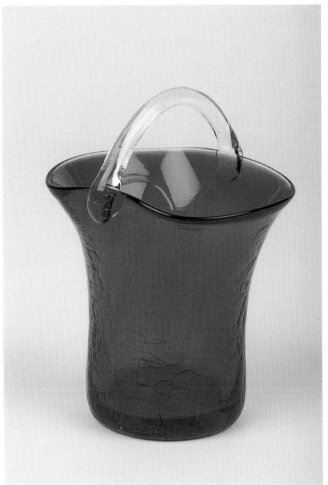

Pilgrim red basket with crystal handle. 4-5/8" h. $15-20

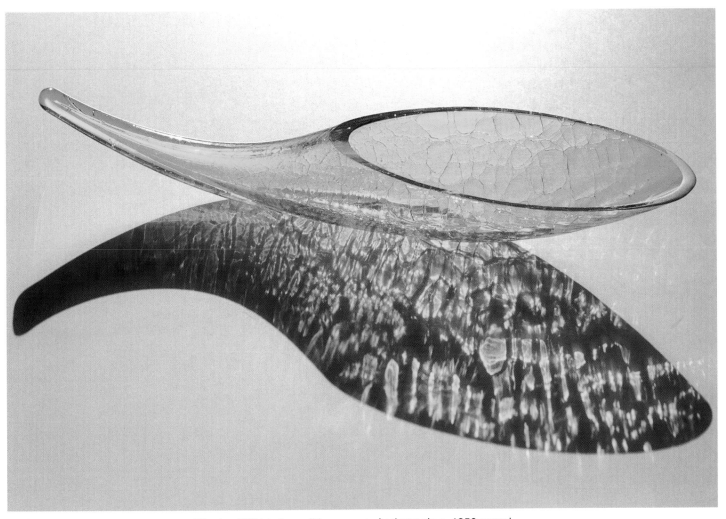

Blenko #964-L Jonquil horn vase, Anderson's c. 1950 award-winning design made in both small (18-1/2") and large sizes. 22" l. *Courtesy of Hansel Jividen.* $100-125

Opposite page:
Top left: Apple with applied leaf, possibly Blenko, but made by several companies. $25-35

Top right: Blue apple with crystal stem, probably Kanawha or Viking. *Courtesy of the Huntington Museum of Art.* $35-45

Bottom: Green fruit with applied leaf, one of many versions of fruit produced in crackle. $35-45

Bibliography

Adkins, Carl. "Roberto Moretti: Carver of Crystal." typescript.

Alford, Judy. *Collecting Crackle Glass*. Atglen, Pennsylvania: Schiffer, 1995.

Corning Museum of Glass. *Glass 1959.* Corning, New York: Corning Museum, 1959.

——— *New Glass: A Worldwide Survey.* Corning New York: Corning Museum, 1979.

"Crackle Glass Heating Up." *Antique Trader's Collector Magazine* (Sept 1996): 7.

Eige, Eason & Rick Wilson. *Blenko Glass: 1930–1953.* Marietta, OH: Antique Publications, 1987.

Eige, Eason. *A Century of Glassmaking in West Virginia.* Huntington, WV: Huntington Galleries, 1980.

——— "Pilgrim's New Cameo Glass." *Glass Collector's Digest* (Oct/Nov 1990):31–37.

Garmon, Lee. "Dalzell–Viking: A Tradition Continues." *Glass Collector's Digest* (Dec/Jan 1990): 30–35.

Goshe, et. al. *Depression Era Stems & Tableware: Tiffin.* Atglen, Pennsylvania: Schiffer, 1998.

Grayson, June. "Crackle Glass." *Glass Collector's Digest* (Oct/Nov 1989): 50–55.

Huntington Galleries. *New American Glass: Focus West Virginia.* Huntington, WV, 1976.

Krause, Gail. "Raymor Modern Connoisseur." *The National Duncan Glass Journal* (Ap/Jun 1983): 4–5.

McKeand, Robert. "A Brief History of the Pilgrim Glass Corporation, Ceredo, West Virginia." typescript, 1986.

McKeand, Robert & Thomas O'Connor. "A Formula for Success: The Pilgrim Glass Story." *Glass Collector's Digest.* (June/July 1992): 35–42.

Miller, Everett R. & Addie R. *The New Martinsville Glass Story.* Marietta, OH: Richardson, 1972.

———*The New Martinsville Glass Story, Book II 1920–1950.* privately printed, 1975.

Piña, Leslie. *Popular '50s & '60s Glass: Color Along the River.* Atglen, Pennsylvania: Schiffer, 1995.

——— *Blenko Glass 1962–1971 Catalogs* . Atglen, Pennsylvania: Schiffer, 2000.

——— *Blenko: Cool '50s & '60 Glass.* Atglen, Pennsylvania: Schiffer, 2000.

"Renowned glass craftsman Roberto Moretti dies at 57." *The Herald Dispatch.* (1986): A1–2.

Rhoads, Betty. "Kanawha Glass." *Glass Collector's Digest* (Feb/Mar 1990): 43–46.

Six, Dean. "Index to Encyclopedia of West Virginia Glass." typescript, 1993.

——— "Kanawha Peachblow." *Glass Collector's Digest* (Oct/Nov 1992): 35–38.

Viking Glass Company. *Beauty is Glass from Viking.* New Martinsville, WV: Viking Glass, 1967.

Wilson, Rick. "We're In For It: Early Days at Blenko Glass." *Goldenseal: West Virginia Traditional Life* 13 (Fall 1987): 43–49.

——— "Blenko Glass: An Inside Story." *Glass Collector's Digest* (Oct/Nov 1987): 73–82.

Index

OTHER SCHIFFER TITLES

Depression Era Art Deco Glass. Leslie Piña & Paula Ockner. Explore American companies which made Art Deco glass during the Depression era: Cambridge, Consolidated, Duncan, Fostoria, Heisey, Libbey, Morgantown, Tiffin, and many others. With more than 350 color photos of popular and rare examples, informative captions with values, patent drawings, company information, a bibliography, and detailed index, this work will delight glass enthusiasts
Size: 8 1/2" x 11" 342 color slides,
49 b & w diagrams   160 pp.
Price Guide/Index
ISBN: 0-7643-0718-5 hard cover $24.95

circa Fifties Glass from Europe & America. Leslie Piña. Here is the Italian and Scandinavian designer art glass usually referred to as "Fifties glass," plus a more popular modern glassware produced in factories, especially in the United States and Italy. This colorful and highly collectible glass is presented with detailed information on 88 designers and makers, design lists for Barovier & Toso and for Venini, glossary, bibliography, and index.
Size: 8 1/2" x 11" 505 photos 216 pp.
Value Guide/Index
ISBN: 0-7643-0229-9 hard cover $49.95

Popular '50s and '60s Glass, Color Along the River. Leslie Piña. Commerical glass production along the Ohio River Valley in the 1950s and 1960s by companies such as Blenko, Pilgrim, Rainbow, Viking, Kanawaha, Bischiff, Morgantown and others that made free- and mold-blown production glass in modern, sometimes bizarre, shapes and wildly vibrant colors. Includes over 400 color photos of the beautiful glass, its labels, catalog pages, and company histories, and a price guide.
Size: 8 1/2" x 11" 409 color photos 176 pp.
Price Guide
ISBN: 0-88740-829-X hard cover $29.95

Fostoria, Serving the American Table 1887-1986. Leslie Piña. A celebration of 100 years of American Fostoria glass, including rarely seen Victorian pattern glass from the early years in Fostoria, Ohio, through the introduction of color, the popular American and Coin patterns, and scarce and unusual, even unique, items. The book contains labels, color catalog pages, an illustrated styles chart with over 1000 entries, a chronology, index, and a price guide.
Size: 8 1/2" x 11" 400+ color photos 192 pp.
Price Guide/Index
ISBN: 0-88740-726-9 hard cover $29.95

Fostoria Designer George Sakier. Leslie Piña. For over fifty years Goerge Sakier sent classic and modern designs to Moundsville, West Virginia, where millions of delightful glass objects were produced. The book includes a thoroughly researched text about the man and his art (paintings, industrial designs and glass), color photos of thousands of Fostoria glass items of many patterns and Sakier's fascinating oil painting landscapes.
Size: 8 1/2" x 11" 380+ photos 176 pp.
Price Guide
ISBN: 0-88740-858-3 hard cover $29.95

Tiffin Glass, 1914–1940. Leslie Piña & Jerry Gallagher. Tiffin was one of the giants of American glassmaking. This is the first book to present all color photos of hundreds of Tiffin's products. Vases, bowls, and candlesticks in a wide variety of colors and styles, from common to rare, are all in this book, with large sections devoted to Tiffin's pressed satin glass, lamps, and baskets.
Size: 8 1/2" x 11" 527 color photos 160 pp.
Price Guide/Index
ISBN: 0-7643-0102-0 hard cover $29.95

Designed & Signed, '50s & '60s Glass, Ceramics & Enamel Wares by Georges Briard, Sascha Brastoff, Marc Bellaire, Higgins. Leslie Piña. Highly collectible household objects designed and signed by name artists of the 1950s and 1960s are presented here including gift and tableware, glass, ceramics and enamel items. Much is written about the leading designer and marketing wizard Georges Briard, and many of his designs are pictured, along with much work by the other prominent featured artists.
Size: 8 1/2 x 11" 587 color photos 192 pp.
Price Guide
ISBN: 0-88740-935-0 hard cover $29.95

Depression Era Glass by Duncan. Leslie Piña. Glassware made by The Duncan & Miller Glass Company, of Washington, Pennsylvania, in the 1920s -1940s is featured. This book presents their Depression Era production and includes essays about their Victorian wares and contribution to the Tiffin Glass Co. Over 500 color photos, catalog pages, advertisements, patent drawings, chronology of company history, detailed captions, bibliography, index, and value guide make this a complete reference for the popular glassware.
Size: 11" x 8 1/2" 457 color photos, 82 b/w images
Price Guide/Index 176 pp.
ISBN: 0-7643-0928-5 hard cover $29.95